from place to PLACE

from place to PLACE
maps and Parish Maps

Edited by
Sue Clifford and Angela King

Common Ground

Published by Common Ground 1996
Seven Dials Warehouse, 44 Earlham Street, London, WC2H 9LA

ISBN: 1 870364 16 3

Designed and typeset on Apple Mac by Stephen Turner and Jane Kendall at Common Ground. Cover image, a detail from 'Parish Map, Old Milverton' © Simon Lewty 1986 collection of the University of Warwick. Printed by Wincanton Print Company in Somerset on Sylvancoat 100% recycled paper.

Common Ground is a registered Charity no. 326335.

This book is available direct from Common Ground @ £10.00 + £1.25 p&p.

Contents

Acknowledgements:

Common Ground is very grateful to all of the contributors for their generosity as well as their insights, everyone has helped us in more ways than are apparent here.Thanks to Simon Lewty for permission to use, on our cover, a detail from the Parish Map of Old Milverton which Common Ground commissioned for the exhibition *Knowing Your Place* in 1986. And our warmest greetings to those who have and are imaginatively creating Parish Maps across the country and beyond, we have learned a lot through your efforts. We hope that everyone will find the disparate essays gathered in this book broadens understanding of the potential.The writers have certainly enabled us to articulate, far better than we can ourselves, the aspirations and achievements so far.

We are most grateful for longstanding support and for help with this book to the Carnegie UK Trust, the London Boroughs Grants Committee and the Countryside Commission.

Foreword

Michael Dower

For each of us, daily life is rooted in a place ... our village, our neighbourhood, our parish or town.

We know what we like about our place; and we may take it for granted ... until someone comes along and threatens its character with, say, a piece of ugly development. But how often do we stop to think what makes the place special for us, and how we could make it even better?

In 1985, Common Ground published 'Holding Your Ground: an action guide to local conservation'. People were inspired to work together in local communities, and it was out of this that the Parish Maps project grew. Over the last ten years hundreds of such maps have been produced, through a wonderful burst of creative energy. Very often, this has led on to positive action to improve the village or the neighbourhood.

Recently, Local Agenda 21 has provoked a fresh round of community action. Parish Maps can help people to agree on what matters about their locality and what action is needed.

The Countryside Commission have been a keen supporter of Common Ground, and of the Parish Maps idea, from the beginning. There is a close link between Parish Maps and our own initiatives to encourage local action or to identify the special character of different areas ... the Rural Action programmes, Parish Paths Partnership, Village Design Statements, and our work on Countryside Character.

I warmly commend this book. I hope that it will inspire you, the reader, to look with fresh eyes at your own familiar place, and to work with and encourage others to celebrate and protect that place.

Michael Dower is Director General of the Countryside Commission

Places, People and Parish Maps

Sue Clifford

Somewhere between the rainbow and the Internet a place that is important to you is struggling to maintain its integrity.

Hundreds of small acts of clairvoyance may precede decisions to pull the hedge out, to build on the allotment, to shut down the factory, to culvert the stream, to cease running the festival, but they are achieved in separate pigeonholes, and their effect each upon the other is hardly ever considered. Rarely is their cumulative impact upon *us* discussed either.

As for the big decisions, arguments which tend to sway politicians and professionals rely on quantifying (how many, how much, how big?), questions about quality and equity which cannot be counted are too difficult, they get marginalised.

How common is it to hear someone say they love a place more because of recent changes, or feel more a part of it? But these should be our aspirations - not to stop change, or to seek to protect only the special things, but - to argue for good surroundings everywhere for all of us. And to work together to achieve more nature, as much history, rich landscape, fit and fitting buildings, as many peoples, the best that our age can offer, in any part of the city and country.

Places are of our manufacture. We and nature conspire, actively or unconsciously, to shift and balance, to accelerate or slow down, to experiment or reiterate. Whatever happens on the World Wide Web, shards of histories, ecologies, economies and cultures are heaped and sifted on bits and pieces of land. Many of us understand ourselves in the world as much through a relationship with a small patch of ground (or more than one) as with people, indeed it is hard to separate them.

The uniqueness of the grid reference is reinforced by the intersection of culture and nature, the sympathy and intensity of their interplay make a place, and endow it with a greater or lesser degree of local distinctiveness.

Local, really local, significance is rehearsed in a subtle dance of detail and patina: we understand a place in close up, through stories retold, meanings shared, accumulations of fragments and identities. Our appreciation of it is often only tested when unsympathetic change threatens, or has already materialised.

But how responsible do we feel for the place and for the changes? All manner of forces bear down upon every inch of soil, every city stone, and despite the intimacy of their impact, many seem beyond our understanding, never mind control. How much courage do we have to summon to stand out against actions we sense will diminish the feel of the place, render it less significant to us in all its intricacies? We are heavily implicated for better or worse. The moment of moving from passive acceptance ("it's such a shame, but what can you do....?") to active engagement ("it could be so much better, what can we do?") can come suddenly in reaction, or slowly as proaction.

Parish Maps

Making a Parish Map is about creating a community expression of values, and about beginning to assert ideas for involvement, it is about taking the place in your own hands.

It begins with, and is sustained by, inclusive gestures and encouraging questions. What is important to you about this place, what does it mean to you? What makes it different from other places? What do you value here? What do we know, what do we want to know? How can we share our understandings? What could we change for the better? Turning each other into experts in this way helps to liberate all kinds of quiet knowledge, as well as passion, about the place. Making a Parish Map can inform, inspire, embolden.

So much surveying, measuring, fact gathering, analysis and policy-making leaves out the very things which make a place significant to the people who know it well. The great thing about making the map yourselves is that you can choose what to put in and what to leave out. You need not be corsetted by convention or conscious of fashion. You can decide on how to gather and discuss, the mix of natural history with buildings, or legends with livelihoods, the scale at which you wish to work, what boundaries to use, the materials, the symbols, the pictures, the words, the place where the map is to hang. You can move at your own pace, be diverted into appearing at a public inquiry, working to clear the footpaths, acting in the community play.... because these are actually the point.

It is the feel of the place which ultimately makes us happy to be there, makes us want to stay, work and play, to engage with it and each other. Social intervention in continually creating and recreating the particularity of a place is not easy, it reminds us that communities are driven by tension as much as compassion, that the fluidity of insiders and outsiders needs constant bridge building, that it is hard work sustaining enthusiasm and effort. The biggest step is the first one - Parish Maps are a way of getting started.

Why Map?

Every day people negotiate their way through known and unfamiliar territory using road, bus and tube maps or the city A-Z. From sketching a meeting place on the back of an envelope to finding a site on the World Wide Web, maps are used as a second language. And few of us can resist sinking into an old chart, with portraits of mountains in soft watercolour, or hachured hills and railways everywhere. The Wind in the Willows, Treasure Island and many more childhood books and films have lured us into pinning down our own dreams or draughting real places in our own hand.

And there is a greater attraction. Seeing the map of Australia printed from their point of view (with north at the bottom, and south at the top), or looking at our familiar atlas made by adventurers from this small archipelago off the coast of Europe, reminds one forcibly that whoever makes the map can choose, and enjoy, central position. A map is an expression of power. It can offer basic information for control: the Ordnance Survey has its origins in visualising the place by - or was it for - the armed forces, hence the name.

Western cartography purports to be factual, conveying a true two dimensional picture of our four/five dimensional world. But, any lover of maps will tell you of the peculiarities and richnesses of charts of different Western cultures, different conventions, endearing or infuriating mistakes, the challenges of updating, and of necessary inaccuracies of representation (if motorways were really as wide as the map portrays...). And increasingly maps are made from satellite recording, ground knowledge is regarded as less precise, less useful, more costly. While we gather ever more facts about the planet, and share incredible amounts of research around the globe, at each extension of scale, detailed place-based knowledge gained over generations is lost, and wisdom mislaid. With each level of abstraction, we feel less able to argue what we know, and less sure in our valuing of the unquantifiable smallnesses which can make everyday life a delight and help nature and culture to interact benignly.

Why Parish?

We are trying to focus on locality, the smallest arena in which life is played out. The territory to which you feel loyalty, which has meaning to you, about which you share some knowledge, for which indignance and protectiveness is easily roused, the neighbourhood of which you have the measure, which in some way helps to shape you.

This is the local, the actual place, where the reference is reality, indifference is unusual, detachment is difficult. Here we are somehow entangled, although we may behave thoughtlessly, responsibility tries to surface. It is here that values and facts act upon each other and are passed on by us to create wisdom about nature, about living, dying and remembering. And more prosaicly, it is where 'strategy' and 'policy' are tested to breaking point.

Y filltir sgwar, bro and cynefin:the Welsh have clung on to ideas which embody more than physical locality - they describe deeply felt ties of familiarity, identification and belonging. *Heimat* in German also carries these meanings. Why have the English never absorbed a word for this, and yet have such strong attachments to places?

It is in this sense of a self defined small territory, that Common Ground has offered the word *parish*, implying people and place together, to keep us grounded. But the origins and other uses of the word are relevant and have proved redolent starting points too.

The ecclesiastical parish has been the measure of the English landscape since Anglo-Saxon times. Boundaries, some dating back more than a thousand years, are often still traceable; here, history marches with nature and each is the richer for the discourse. This tracery may be tangible in the city as the curving line of a street, or in the country as the double bank and ditch dancing with butterflies. For although dynamism is an identifying feature of nature, broad continuity creates the conditions for the changes to build each on the other, species to diversify, ecosystems to mature.

The civil parish emerged in the 1890s as the smallest theatre of democracy. Much has changed since then: boundaries have been reworked, and in the city the ward does not have the same ring, community councils in Wales and Scotland encompass but do not imply territory. More of us have the right to vote, yet less of us are voting. Desperation for better decisions parallels cynicism for politicians. Weaving a 21st century environment and society has to be about constructing a more participative and pliable democracy too.

Parish Maps again
This book offers just a few fragmented insights into the potential powers of working with maps. Parish Maps have been promoted by Common Ground as a lively way of socially exploring and demonstrating what people value in their own place, and as a means to generating and liberating enthusiasms for doing something.

Knowing your place, taking some active part in its upkeep, passing on wisdom, being open to ideas, people, development, change but in sympathy with nature and culture which have brought it this far, will open the doors of dissent. But conversation, tolerance and the passing on of memories, are civilising forces. Whatever the forms of knowledge we shall need for the next millennium, humanity and imagination must take a high priority in organising them.

In making a Parish Map you can come together to hold the frame where you want it to be, you can throw light on the things which are important to you, and you may find courage to speak with passion about why all this matters.

The rainbow is as 'virtual' as anything yet imagined by the software wizards, and yet in touching the ground it briefly holds both the intangible and the physical together, it frames, focusses and reminds us of the enchantment and reality of our small world.

Sue Clifford is a Founder Director of Common Ground

Parish Maps: Local Knowledge and the reconstitution of democracy

Robin Grove-White

Common Ground's Parish Maps are a modest idea - but an idea with a very big future. I want to argue that this apparently simple notion, of members of a local community 'mapping' for themselves what they value about their 'place', contains vital pointers for how our politics generally are going to have to develop as we enter the millennium.

Parish Maps as a central tool in the politics of advanced industrial society? Is that not fanciful, in an era of globalisation and the Internet? I think not - though explaining why requires a brisk journey into the sociological undergrowth of recent developments in democracies like ours.

The success of Common Ground's Parish Maps so far has rested on the fact that they are creative enterprises to which everyone can contribute. They invite people to say what it is they value about where they live, and to share with one another the processes of representing this on a map. So Parish Maps are personal and intimate, at the same time as being expressions of *collective* endeavour and concern, generated outside 'official' frameworks. They permit people to devise *their own* and shared categories of meaning and priority about 'the local', and to express these in permanent graphic forms that others can acknowledge.

Public authorities have tended so far to see the results as attractive but *soft*. That has been perhaps a predictable reflection of those bodies' commitment to specialist technical vocabularies of their own - 'structure plans', 'growth envelopes', 'areas of landscape importance', and the like. Alongside the well-honed 'objective' plans, procedures and vocabularies of the Land Use Planning system, Parish Maps may appear beguiling but irredeemably subjective. Perhaps they are seen as helpful expressions of grass-roots opinion, but their practical utility to the grown-up official world of 'strategic planning' and 'development control' has so far appeared limited.

All that is about to change. Parish Maps are an idea whose time has come.

By all the appearances, we are a society of growing discontent and disharmony. The old symbols and mechanisms - the monarchy, Parliament, local government, the inner confidence of being 'British' - are corroding fast. The old securities - of job, of social welfare, even of class - are no longer guaranteed. Such changes are happening so fast, and so cumulatively, that it is hard for most of us to make sense of them.

Sociologists like Antony Giddens, Zygmundt Bauman and Ulrich Beck point in their different ways to the *novelty* of our situation in advanced industrial societies. The dynamism and increasing pervasiveness of global capitalism means that we are now on a roller-coaster of accelerating change, whether or not we acknowledge it. Not everyone may want weekend holiday breaks in Thailand, or lucrative insecure employment in 'downsized' trans-national companies, or the new world Rugby league on satellite TV, but these are reflections of forces in which we are all now embedded - forces that simultaneously are fragmenting old patterns of identification, and contriving to generate new ones in their place.

Nor are we simply passive 'victims' of such processes. In important respects, they are expressions of how we ourselves are now evolving - even of how we *want* to be. This is an era of individuals. To some such a development has only bad connotations - the 'Thatcherite individualism' of the 1980s for example is alleged to have been uniquely corrosive of vital social bonds. But for others - echoed by social analysts such as Ray Pahl, Robert Bellah and Bron Szerzsynski - there are also grounds for cautious optimism; the forces of change reflect for many people a flowering of individuality, which, unlike the self-centredness of individualism, is permitting new forms of shared aspiration and concern to begin to crystallise, forms of common value which may well be more appropriate for our times than their antecedents.

Today's universal concern with 'the environment' is a striking case in point. If ever there was a grass-roots cultural movement developed in defiance of orthodox political categories and understandings, environmentalism has been it. Over the past two or three decades, 'the environment' emerged as a grass-roots rallying-point - not only for a range of shared discontents about aspects of modern industrialism, but also for fresh ways of beginning to picture elements of a more harmonious social order, appropriate to the new 'global' circumstances.

Since the early 1990s, as the official post-Rio vocabulary of 'sustainable development' indicates, environmentalism has itself begun to become political orthodoxy. In one sense this has represented success for the social movement of the 1970s and 1980s. In another, such an outcome has been bought at a price. Through processes of political elision, the spontaneous common concerns embodied in environmentalism are now being domesticated, in attempts to make them digestible for purposes of public administration, nationally and internationally.

But the forces involved are impossible to contain in this way. At the very moment when governments have begun to adopt these new vocabularies, environmentalism has been spawning new mutations - novel patterns of grass-roots protest and direct action about roads and animal welfare, new challenges to accomodations between economic interests and government (Brent Spar et al), new concerns about regional culture and place, and a growing popular consciousness of risk and uncertainty in everyday life, of the kind manifested in recent BSE crises. All of this is consistent with the experience of the past twenty years. Environmentalism has emerged and crystallised as a DIY response to chronically felt limitations in the responsiveness of our political institutions. That role continues.

One further feature of the contemporary British polity should be mentioned, before the potential future significance of all this for Common Ground's Parish Maps can be understood. This concerns the spate of 'reforms' now under way in this country within the machinery of government itself - particularly the civil service. A slow revolution is gathering speed in Whitehall, the likely consequences of which are impossible fully to predict. Paralleling the wave of privatisations of public utilities in the late 80s and early 90s, increasing numbers of functions of government are now being hived off to new executive agencies ("Next Steps Agencies" and the like) or directly to the private sector. A striking direct consequence is the emergence in Britain of what Michael Power has termed the new 'audit culture' in our public domain - an ungainly matrix of 'objective setting', 'performance targets', 'customers' and 'quantitative indicators'. Collectively, these notions are now playing an accelerating role in shaping the priorities and behaviours of an ever-greater proportion of the working population.

Whatever the claimed merits of such changes for 'efficient policy delivery', there is already enough experience of them for one unambiguous conclusion to be drawn. They are not processes which favour a more sensitive official understanding of people's patterns of *intimate personal* experience of contemporary social change. The pursuit of instrumental efficiency and value for money may well be admirable in themselves, but, as Brian Wynne, Michael Jacobs and others have pointed out, they rest on a highly restricted conception of human needs and aspiration. In this sense, the recent reforms within government may be encouraging official myopia and ignorance on matters of great human importance, even while they (apparently) balance the books.

So how are we to interpret these overall developments? My suggestion is that, at a time of pervasive social and cultural change, people are striving to adapt and to assert new forms of shared value, in ways which government and its agencies may no longer be equipped to understand. Repeated recent opinion surveys show the unnerving extent of public scorn for Westminster and local politicians. Almost certainly these gaps are contributing to the current burgeoning sense of a need for constitutional reform in Britain.

And Parish Maps have a role in what comes next.

Growing numbers of local authorities and public agencies are now becoming conscious of the need to relate more closely to the publics they claim to serve and represent. However, there is an emerging body of evidence that points to the alienating character of the official idioms in which many such participation initiatives are tending to be framed. For example, recent studies undertaken for Lancashire County Council and DOE's Biodiversity Action Plan Steering Group point to gaps between official 'sustainable development' discourses (within Local Agenda 21, or biodiversity initiatives) and ordinary people's understanding and experience of relevant problems and issues in their own lives. Such tensions appear to reflect the wider patterns of public mistrust and fatalism evident in the UK vis a vis the claims to good faith of political parties and other public institutions.

Addressing such corrosion of popular identification with institutions whose claims to legitimacy have rested precisely on their ability to 'represent' the public is becoming recognised as a major challenge for society as a whole. One conclusion seems obvious: such reconstitution of trust and interdependency will be likely to emerge not from top-down *pronunciamentos* from central government, so much as from the careful rebuilding of shared understanding of public values from the *ground up*. Indeed, it is precisely the attraction of Local Agenda 21 that it offers a framework within which such essentially creative processes may begin to be fostered.

It is in this context that the Parish Maps idea holds promise of far-reaching significance. For the Parish Map is a device resting above all on respect for the affective *meanings* of 'community' and nature, for ordinary people on the ground. It is a medium, in short, for harnessing 'local' knowledge of many kinds. Such maps reject, deliberately, the etiolated instrumental and 'objective' categories and vocabularies of even enlightened bureaucratic discourse, making explicit instead dimensions of human experience which such discourse tends systematically to sideline or, worse still, to ignore. Common Ground's insights concerning the significance of the intimate, the relational, and the locally valued, and the ways in which these can be expressed and reflected in Parish Maps, thus hold considerable potential for the burgeoning wider process of reinvigoration of democratic politics, in the circumstances of an advanced industrial society like Britain.

Let us build on such devices, and the respect for human sensibility they embody, to enrich the ways in which we are to organise ourselves, as the millennium approaches.

References

Bauman, Z. *Intimations of Post Modernity*, Routledge, 1991.

Beck, U. *Risk Society: Towards a New Modernity*, Sage, 1992.

Bellah, R. et al *Habits of the Heart: Individualism and Commitment in American Life*, University of California Press, 1985.

Giddens, A. *The Consequences of Modernity*, Polity, 1994.

Grove-White, R. 'Environmental Knowledge and Public Policy Needs: On Humanising the Research Agenda', in Lash, S, Szerszynski, B & Wynne, B eds. *Risk, Environment and Modernity*, Sage, 1996.

Jacobs, M. 'The limits to Neo-Classicism', in Redclift, M & Benton, T eds. *Social Theory and the Global Environment*, Routledge, 1994.

Macnaghten, P. et al *Public Perceptions of Sustainability in Lancashire*, Lancashire County Council, 1995.

Pahl, R. *Friendly Society,* New Statesman & Society, 10 March 1995

Pollock, J. *"Bio-Whatever": Science, Art and Life in the Public Engagement of Environmental Issues.* Unpublished Report to the Department of the Environment (DOE) Biodiversity Action Plan Steering Group, DOE, 1995.

Power, M. *The Audit Explosion*, Demos, 1994.

Szerszynski, B. *The Politics of Dependence*, paper presented to Politics of Cultural Change conference, Lancaster Centre for the Study of Environmental Change, 1994.

Wilkinson, H. & Mulgan, G. *Freedom's Children: Work, Relationships and Politics for 18-34 year olds in Britain today*, Demos, 1995.

Wynne, B. 'May the Sheep Safely Graze? A Reflexive View of the Expert-Lay knowledge Divide', in Lash S. Szersynski, B. & Wynne, B. - *Risk, Environment and Modernity*, Sage, 1996.

Robin Grove-White is director of the Centre for the Study of Environmental Change at Lancaster University.

The Short Cut and the Long Way Round

Richard Mabey

After so many mild winters, I had forgotten how dramatically snow redraws the map. Everything shallow and insubstantial in the landscape - flat roads, bramble patches, crops - simply vanishes. All that are left are the gaunt fundamentals of tree, hill and ditch. But the snow itself then becomes a blank sheet for a new kind of chart, that sketches out the ephemeral routeways and land-uses of myriads of creatures. In the big fields below my wood, badger tracks leave the chalk scrub and fan out across the snow. They are full of curves and subtle kinks - exactly like the trail made by my own footprints when I look behind me. However hard you try it is impossible to walk in an unguided straight line between two points. When you do not even try, your track becomes a bewildering zig-zag of pauses, diversions, back-trackings, and of expeditions over tracts of land you would not dream of straying onto in the summer. (I once discovered a long-lost trackway in my wood simply because the snow provided a fresh way of seeing a gap through the trees I'd glanced at and ignored a hundred times before.)

I am intrigued by the notion that all places have alternative, undrawn charts like this - 'maps in the head', so to speak, that record the way we cope with topography when free of the promptings of trackways and boundaries. And maybe the prompting of our own ingrained habits, too. I get shamefaced sometimes when I think of how unadventurous I can be in my own meanderings. Like William Hazlitt, I tend to follow my own footsteps on familiar walks, "stopping and turning to look back, and thinking to strike off into less trodden paths, yet hesitant to quit the one I am on, afraid to snap the brittle threads of memory." A rut is sometimes a good thing to follow, but not to be stuck in. One odd feature of this is that almost all my habitual walks are done clockwise. I always perambulate the ancient beech pollards at Frithsden clockwise; leave town along the canal and come home up on the ridgeway; make a loop through the water meadows of the Chess at Chenies and return through the beechwood where the coralroot grows. The only exception, the one walk I invariably do anti-clockwise, is the circumnavigation of my wood - and there I am following a brand-new track we made ourselves.

Perhaps this curious rotational habit has some deep psychological or geographical root, like Thoreau's inclination to walk westward, following the sun and the expanding frontier. But what I am really thinking of here is the way in which the landscape itself becomes a prompt when you are away from properly mapped routes. I know that I am tugged this way and that by gaps in the hedge, intriguing plant tufts, faces imagined in tree trunks, and barely comprehended signals from bushes and rocks. But what else, and why? There are two places I walk that don't have much in the way of official pathways, but where I have strong memories of the routes I've taken.

The great sweep of common land between Ashridge and Berkhamsted has plenty of bridleways and broad footpaths, but also a catacomb of unmarked deer and rabbit tracks through the bracken. Whenever I am there the urge to potter always overcomes any vestigial intention to 'get somewhere'. I'm drawn to self-sown oaks, for instance, and searching for ceps or seedlings under them, depending on the season. And to a marooned clump of aspens, whose precise location I can never remember until I've hunted around amongst the birches. Dense thorn clumps are always magnets, as is anything that looks remotely like an overgrown pond. Sometimes I try to be clever and see if I can get back on deer-tracks alone, without beating any new ways through the bracken. But halfway back, the sun comes out, and I find myself walking in a totally different direction, to a thin strip of hanging beechwood at the common's edge with an unequalled south-facing view of the town.

The same habit - a kind of ambulatory doodling - is even more pronounced on a walk I have been doing annually for nearly thirty years. Blakeney Point is a 4-mile-long ridge of sand and tide-thrown shingle that encloses one of the most magical bays in eastern England. It is an exhausting plod on the bare pebbles, like walking on a treadmill, and the saltmarsh that lies inland from the spit is not much easier. It is fretted with deep creeks, and barred here and there by tongues of shingle that have been sprayed into the marsh by storm tides. I usually start on the shingle, then take to the marsh for some kind of relief. There are special places to stop, that need their own detours. One gives a view of the string of coastal villages the other side of Blakeney Harbour. Another overlooks a mud-flat where waders congregate as the tide rises. From this vantage point everything seems to be moving - yachts in the harbour, bird flocks, even plants bending with the current. I tend to lose myself in the tide-watching, gazing at them much as one does at a fire, watching for the point of turning, for those damp runnels of sand to emerge scoured and sculptured in shapes that have never existed before.

I try to walk back along the marshland edge, but it is often impossible. There are new pools everywhere. The rough tracks are covered with flashes of water and scuttling crabs, which shape up to me with their claws as I pass. Trying to keep dry and show a bit of marsh savvy, I hop from island to island - and go repeatedly up to my knees in hidden creeks. A bird's-eye-view of my route through the tideline debris of flotsam, seablight bushes, dead birds and shells would, I suspect, have the same labyrinthine pattern as the network of creeks eaten out by the sea.

There are two institutions that socialise these private and seemingly random strollings. The Short-Cut is a piece of vernacular and often personal knowledge, which has less to do with cutting distances than demonstrating landscape expertise. The Long Way Round (or Detour) is more aesthetic and meditative, a way of savouring - and sharing - secret local high spots. Both are part of an oral tradition, passed down through families or gangs, and echo our relict, animal sense of territory. Neither feature on conventional maps but exemplify that special kind of local knowledge that is the foundation of Parish Maps.

Richard Mabey is a writer and broadcaster on our relationships with nature.

Maps

Adam Nicolson

Both landscapes and maps - or at least the usual kind of map you can buy in the post office or newsagents - have what you might call an 'emergent beauty' about them. In both, the beautiful is not usually the intended thing. For the landscape, at least the farmed landscape, the intention is always to make a house that suits, a barn that protects, a field that can be cultivated, a hedge that contains the stock, a wood that grows the wood, even a moor that nurtures the grouse or the deer. Beauty emerges from these things; it is not their purpose.

You might even say that if there is one thing which does not work in landscapes it is the obvious striving after the beautiful effect. If somewhere slaps you over the face with the slogan 'I am Beautiful, Look at Me', the meaning will be somehow sterilised and the place coarsened. It is like someone shouting. You turn away, looking for something whose allure is, at least apparently, unconscious.

For a landscape to be beautiful, its richer meanings must steal up on you, seeping unheard from the pores of the seen. The most successful consciously designed landscapes are those which mimic this strange, absent-minded quality, as though the design and the designer were not all-powerful in front of what they were given. The landscape itself, before they redesigned it, continues to speak after they have done. Their work does not encompass everything the place has to offer. There is, somehow, a residual essence, beyond the intentional.

That is also the beauty of maps. One of the reasons that maps can resonate so richly with us is their double description of place. Not only, with every intention and every acuity finely tuned, do they map out the substance of the known, precisely delineating the actual facts of field, wood, orchard and road. Not only do they locate and orientate with a precision which is almost unreasonably tight. They do that other thing which landsapes do themselves: they allow the beauty of place to come leaking unintentionally out through the surface, like the mist rising in the early morning on the grasses of a riverside meadow. Read a map and you are looking at the flow lines and the stopping places of people over immense lengths of time, the gridding of space by history. Read a map and you are holding a landscape, its infinite connectedness, its lack of a linear strait-jacket, in your richly privileged hand.

Mapping is one of the markers of civilisation. It is, almost in a physical sense, a sign of breadth of mind. It extends understanding beyond the ploddingly sequential. A line of text like this one is an avenue: you start at one end and you drive straight down its inescapable path to the other. But a map is a wood, a mazy wriggle-zone in which the eye and mind wander into the netted reality of place. You can, of course, select your track and follow that line. But the reality of the map, its beauty and its richness, is the grid, its squareness, its multiplying of meanings.

I live on a small farm in the Sussex Weald. It is a beautiful place but it has been driven hard over the last forty years or so. The landscape here is in need of mending and we are slowly, quite tentatively, beginning that process. A happy conclusion and an air of completeness seem at times a long way off. There are moments when I look out at some of the concrete and barbed wire wreckage and think that wholeness will not come back here.

But the other day I saw a picture of what this place might one day be, I was in the University Library in Cambridge. The library is, in its way, a hideously heroic building, sharing its architect with Battersea Power Station, and you can see the family relation. Despite that, it's one of the most wonderful places I know, not for what it looks like but for what it contains. Walking around its mile on mile of sterilised, ugly, half-warehouse, half-lunatic asylum corridors, you know that you are walking around the world mind. Everything is there. Any hidden corner of any forgotten esotericism is to hand, up a lift, down the ugly passage, quietly biding its time, lurking in the library's semi sub-conscious depths.

Falling asleep over what I was meant to be reading, I decided to see if Perch Hill Farm featured in the world mind. There was nothing in the computer catalogue, but that was probably too much to expect, so I went to the Map Room. Here on giant green tables a serious man, writing the history of Bechuanaland in the late 1890s, pores over garish maps of mineral deposits and catchment areas; a woman in an

Inca-style cardigan is analysing the hydrography of Scapa Flow; I ask for Perch Hill Farm. "Certainly," the map librarian says. "Just fill in the form". She disappears for a minute or two while I kick my heels and she returns with one heavily and precisely folded piece of paper.

She leaves me to it and carefully I unfold the sheet. It is large, perhaps three feet by two, and has a clean and precise air to it, as if freshly laundered. There is even the smell, in its inner sections, of newness and ink. But it is far from new. This map is part of the great 25 inches to the mile series made in the second half of the 19th century. This particular sheet was produced in 1898. I don't think anyone has looked at it since it was made.

At my own giant green table, I pore over the map of home. The farm just about fills the sheet. The other people may be thinking about, analysing or drawing conclusions from the maps in front of them. I'm not. I'm in bed with my map, loving every inch of it, drinking it up, reading the reality of hedge-bend, gateway, wood-corner and stream-turn, surveyed so exactly, drawn so carefully, displayed so perfectly in front of me. This map series, which marks individual trees in hedges and names every field, which if laid out for the whole country would stretch 200 yards from the Lizard to the Cheviots, scarcely less from Southwold to St David's, is probably the greatest map ever made.

I look at my sheet, one tessera of a stadium-size mosaic, and in it see the state of perfection, described in a fortnight's work in the spring of 1898: the hop-garden in Hollow Flemings, no longer there; the small wood that cuts in two the big field known as Great Flemings, no longer there; the three hedges that make small compartments of the other big hay meadow, the Way Field, none of them now there; the little wood dividing Target from Cottage Field, marked now only by a bank and a single oak; the orchard in the Cottage Field, of which one fruitless plum tree remains.

Here, in the Map Room, surrounded by the nearly audible sound of the collective Cambridge brain ticking, I see something else: this place in its rich, divided wholeness, the picture a century ago, the agenda for the next 40 years.

Adam Nicolson is a writer and journalist.

'One Little Room, an Everywhere'

Roger Deakin

Ellis Martin's illustration for the cover of the old 1919 edition of the one-inch Ordnance Survey map shows a pipe-smoking Glen Baxter type in shirt-sleeves and pullover seated with knapsack on a grassy hillside vantage point studying a map of the countryside beyond. This is a generalised landscape with storybook woodland, a glimpse of river and bridge in the valley below, distant steeple, and far-off cliffs and sea. The idyll invites us to step in through its oak-garlanded frame and identify with this questing, leisured figure.

The map before him is the kind that suggests where you are going *to*, and it is quite distinct from another kind of map altogether; the map of where you come *from*.

Parish Maps, like the original Mapa Mundi, naturally fall into the second category. The Mapa Mundi was a mythic map showing the world as people imagined it; it showed where they were'coming from'; but it wouldn't have been much use for a circumnavigation. Only later did maps succumb to the common man's need for something more practical; something for the sea-discoverers, merchants and navigators.

The ambiguity of any map is implicit in the term 'map-reading'. Until we bring our imagination to bear upon it, the map is simply a collection of marks on paper, so the act of reading is a collaborative, creative process. How you read a map thus depends very much on your own internal limits. There is a world of difference between a trip (essentially a loop, ending where you began), and a voyage. A voyage knows no limits, and suits a quite different state of mind. It is described in the sonnet Keats wrote 'On first looking into Chapman's Homer':

Then felt I like some watcher of the skies
When a new planet swims into his ken;
Or like stout Cortez when with eagle eyes
He star'd at the Pacific - and all his men
Look'd at each other with a wild surmise -
Silent, upon a peak in Darien.

The man on the front of the Ordnance Survey map could well be experiencing just such feelings; indeed he looks a bit like George Orwell, an adventurer in his native land like Cobbett before him. A few years ago I went exploring on Jura, the Hebridean island where Orwell lived and farmed towards the end of his life. I climbed to the top of one of the three Paps, the mountains that loom over the island. True to the Ordnance Survey spirit, I wrote in my notebook:

I could now see the whole island; a mass of brown, purple and green contours thrown into sharp, crinkly relief by the black shadows and the dazzling sunshine, like an atlas. And immediately I could see where I wanted to go, descending along the river to Glenbatrick Bay and the solitary house by the white sands. I sat in the sun for half an hour in a state of extreme bliss - I could happily have stayed up there all day. I could see Ireland, and across the glinting sea to Colonsay and all the other isles beyond, all the way to Lewis. Looking north again, I noticed the treacherous Gulf of Corryvreckan, which separates Jura from Scarba. It was here, in 1947, that Orwell was shipwrecked when he miscalculated the tides and took his boat into the whirlpool that lurks between the two islands.

I find this interesting now not so much as an objective description of the place but for its subjectivity, as a description of what George Eliot calls (in 'Daniel Deronda') 'The unmapped country within'. My internal response to Jura had been conditioned by seeing Peter Brook's production of 'The Tempest' only two days earlier in Glasgow, by reading about Orwell's life on the island, by having in my rucksack a copy of another work of island fiction, Marianne Wiggins' 'John Dollar', and by being cheerfully in love.

I had fallen in love with Jura too, seeing it for the first time earlier that summer across the water from a kind of honeymoon hut on a promontory on the mainland. I desired the island, therefore I desired to explore and describe it, mapping it in my imagination long before I set foot on it, and long after I left. Perhaps love of a place, as with love of another person, can be just as paradoxical in widening the imagination through the very narrowing of focus. This is the metaphysical notion famously expressed by John Donne in 'The Good Morrow':

For love all love of other sights controules
And makes one little room, an everywhere.
Let sea-discoverers to new worlds have gone
Let Maps to other, worlds on worlds have showne,
Let us posesse one worlde, each hath one, and is one.

An island, or a parish, accomodates to the imagination because it is framed or contained (like a 'little room') by the sea or by ancient boundaries, natural and supernatural. what might seem limiting and defining to one state of mind can be at once liberating to another. The richness of our island literature from 'Robinson Crusoe' and 'Coral Island' to 'Lord of the Flies' and 'John Dollar' suggests the potency of the metaphor.

Approaching Jura, still steeped in 'The Tempest', as a magical island, words on the map took poetic effect on my suggestible mind. the map cryptically mentions "raised beaches". The words recur like an incantation, forming a ribbon along the north western shores reminiscent of the words repeated on David Nash's parish map of Blaenau Ffestiniog; 'quarry', 'path', 'crag', 'granite', 'bog', 'grass', so that the map literally speaks to us. The effect is similar to the quality Macaulay observed in Milton's verse when he said "Its merit lies less in its overt meaning than in its occult power."

There is no doubting the occult power of a raised beach, a ridge of big, smooth, pale grey, purple-veined pebbles, like curling stones or loaves, rising between ten and thirty feet from the sea shore all along Jura's north-west coastline. A monument to centuries of giant waves roughing up the island, trying to flip it over the wrong way up. The island responded by throwing up huge wet-stone ramparts. On top of them, generations of ants founded ant-hills that grew to the size of small tumuli as they built on the ruins of their forbears. The heather, moss and bilberries took root in the fertile ant-compost, and deer nibbled them to a close-cropped topiary, like green thatched roofs.

Perhaps there is a name for these striking ant-works, but I am happy to say that it is not on the map, for even more magical than names are all the mysteries and wonders that attach to what the Greeks call 'The unwritten places'. The 'Agrafa'. These are the remote, secret places in the Pindos mountains that were never written on the map so as to avoid the imposition of taxes by the occupying Turks. Patrick Kavanagh beautifully describes his attachment to such things in his poem 'On Reading a Book of Common Wild Flowers':

I knew them all by eyesight long before I knew their names.
We were in love before we were introduced.

Recognition, re-cognition, is a creative art that involves the memory and our own internal map of places, objects and people. It usually involves the affections too. Those ant-works are on a map; the invisible, collective map of anyone who has noticed them and delighted in them as I have. We can recognise a map like an old friend; and an old friend like a map. In both instances, the sum of the features is a subtle language we may never fully understand. The human face, the portal of the soul, is a map we never tire of studying, and Paris, with its pavement cafes and restless eyes, is a whole city of map-readers. Stephen Spender, in his memorial address on W. H. Auden, described him thus:

The second image of Wystan is of course the one with which you are all familiar: the famous poet with a face like a map of physical geograpy, criss-crossed and river-run and creased with lines. This was a face upon which experiences and thoughts had hammered; a face of isolated self-communing which reminded me of a phrase of Montherlant's about the artist's task of 'noble self-cultivation'; a face that was still somehow entertaining and which could break down into a smile of benevolence or light up with gratified recognition at some anecdote recounted or thought received. It was a face at once armoured and receptive.

Spender could well have been describing some ancient landscape. It is like Maria's description of Malvolio in 'Twelfth Night'; *He does smile his face into more lines than is in the new map with the augmentation of the Indies.* Here is a map being drawn out of love; a map of a man whose favourite personal landscape was remarkably like his own complicated face:

Tramline and slagheaps, pieces of machinery
That was, and still is, my scenery,

Because the 'scenery' expresses the soul of the place, we say it is its 'face', as you might say "the face of Kirkby Lonsdale". Like a portrait, a Parish Map can express the interior world of a place and its people - its unwritten places - and be the more truthful. You have to stare at something over and over again, in the words of Freud, until it speaks to you. The fishermen at the Cliffs Cafe in Overstrand near Cromer seem to know about this. They keep a windscreen wiper on the sill of the big steamed-up bay window to clear the condensation and gaze out to sea.

Like Auden's face, the world is 'both armoured and receptive', still full of mysteries. There *is* still a new world waiting for us to discover, but it is not the one to which the 'sea-discoverers' have gone. Like the things in a novel which are left unsaid, it is the gaps between words, the unsung, the unwritten places that haunt the imagination.

Jura, and the waters around the Corryvreckan whirlpool, were favourite 'haunts' of Orwell, and now he haunts these places, lending them a heightened, mythic fascination. Wordsworth talks about 'haunting spots of time', memories, things, places waiting for the chance connection that will spring them vividly into the imagination. The psychoanalyst Wilfrid Bion relates just such a moment when a friend, leaning over a field gate in Warwickshire in the 1930s and passing the time of day with an old farm labourer, remarks on the profusions of dandelions in the field, some in flower, and some already gone to seed. The old man refers to them as 'golden lads and girls', and to the dandelion 'clocks' as 'chimney-sweeps'. Bion's friend, a Shakespeare scholar, is astonished thus to learn at last the meaning of two lines in the song in 'Cymbeline' that had long puzzled him:

Golden lads and girls all must
As chimney-sweepers come to dust.

He immediately reflects that Shakespeare may have looked on the same fields, that these are his Warwickshire haunts. He has stumbled upon one of the unwritten places.

Roger Deakin is a writer and a film maker.

Looking for the Burren

Tim Robinson

A map that is intended as a graphic expression of a sense of place - one person's sense of one place - has to face the question of the unity of the place: given this name 'The Burren', so compact, tough and resonant, to find a worthy domain for it. Historically it is the name of a Barony, the ancient territory of the O'Lochlainns whose descendents are to be met with around Ballyvaughan. The word *boireann* means a rocky place; the rock in question is limestone, and much of the Barony is of a strikingly bare and craggy landform which gives the region its core of individuality, though not, I think, its fully rounded definition..

This map proposes a Burren more extensive than the Barony, but still restricted to the uplands: the hills that look north onto Galway Bay, west out to Aran and east across the Gort plain, together with the plateau they half encircle. With its natural and undogmatic frontiers in the Aille and upper Fergus valleys, this is an aesthetically defensible territory. Shale or limestone, its surfaces are visually one; it commends itself to a sheet of paper. I have included just enough of the valleys and the Corofin lakeland levels (an area with its own intense individuality) to serve as a background against which the unity of this particular Burren may stand out.

A characteristic gesture of the skyline indicates this region. The hillsides lift from seashore or valley in a smooth curve up to a certain height, above which they rise in giant steps. The lower strata of limestone tend to form smooth slopes, whereas the more massively bedded upper strata tend to form terraces separated by low cliffs. The division, a spring-line, is marked by a band of clay which can be traced all round the region. From the visual point of view, after the shale boundary it is the most important line to be read in the palm of the Burren. The terraces above it march like grand processional ways around the northern hills. Towards the south-east where the strata underwent more folding before the hills were carved out of them, the same terraces become wildly swinging helterskelters, around Sliabh Rua and the Mullach Mór....

The Burren could almost be defined by its rich concentration of archaeological sites. The Survey of Megalithic Tombs of 1961 shows a close grouping of 66 of these graves of the earliest settlers, nearly all wedge-graves of a local form they owe to the natural limestone slabs produced by the rectangular fissuring of the region... At a rough count I have marked 450 ringforts and similar enclosures on the limestone (for comparison, there are around 800 houses); the little circles on the map can only lure you to the spot, they cannot convey the number of interesting ways in which these old homesteads are returning to the earth. As even the most decayed and scarcely traceable of them may reveal something of the past, poetically or archaeologically, I have omitted none that I could make out at all....

Cahers and burial mounds have been preserved by a belief that they are fairy forts. The superstition is not to be dismissed; its core is a proper reverence before the mystery of the past, and this land is full of questions that only a respectful attention to its ancient stones can ever answer. Nobody knows the origins, perhaps prehistoric, of the melancholy and beautiful little cillín graveyards for unbaptised children. The huge summit cairn of Turlough Hill may or may not be a Bronze Age cemetery like the smaller cairn of Poulawack. The graves of Crocán na Spáinneach may be more recent. Local tradition alone identifies the tiny secret chapel of the penal times in Formoyle. The forgotten church up in Sladoo dates from - when? A clue to the bitterness of the last century is to be found on the hillsides south of Ballyallaban and on Gleninagh Mountain - narrow U-shaped drystone enclosures in which cowdung and sods peeled off the rock were stored and dried as fuel. Ruins of corbelled stone huts of indeterminate age are common on the uplands, and the tiny versions of them in which goat-kids are reared. Slabs of stone like hands or figures or crosses have been jammed upright in fissures of the weird crags around Poulbaun; are they memorials to anything other than the tedium of the herdsman's life?

This map is organised by the sense of sight; I cannot see Time (as a good historian can) and the dates of buldings and events I have noted do not begin to compose a local history; they mark, though, some points of attachment of the historical web, from which one can grope back along the strands into the darkness. And what a terrible darkness much of it is! Let me mention here what is omitted, for this map is haunted by the hundreds of roofless cottages I have crossed off my copies of the old survey. Famine half emptied the land in the last century; the hazel scrub has spread and swallowed up whole villages as well as great stone cahers. Now the bulldozer is called in to rescue the land, and the last traces of a community are swept away - hearth, path, field and well.

I was glad to discover that the two small hills I have taken as the northern and southern limits of the Burren are both called by the same diminutive, *boirnín*, little Burren. Everywhere, the land speaks of itself and its history through its placenames. And history has dealt curiously with the placenames of regions like this, depriving them of the support of a written language, leaving them in the still pools of an oral culture. The 19th century surveyors chose to endorse the practise of writing Irish names in English phonetics, and having taken that wrong turn were driven into absurdity after absurdity by the demon of consistency. What is to be done? The townland names have become familiar and official in their anglicised forms, but hundreds of other places whose memory is not mediated by map or deed are still known by Irish names, and to record these in a form that stunts the sound and stifles the sense should no longer be permissable, especially in this area with its recent memory of Irish in general use, and in the presence of the living language at Gleninagh. Such names are presented here in standard spelling. Wherever possible I have used a minor name to give the sense of the original of the anglicised townland name. Some of these Irish names were given me by local people, others are from the writings of Westropp, Frost, the Ordnance Survey Letters and in particular the Field Name Books of the first survey. Naturally these authorities often disagree, and a shadow of a question mark hangs about a few of these versions, while the testimony of other names is irrecoverable.

The present reawakening and self-discovery of the Burren is very evident. The dates of new schools, buildings and institutions I have noted seem to press forward into the future. As the 'rocky place' feels the tremor of change, the image I have to offer is already that of a moment in its richly interwoven past.

With thanks for permission to quote extracts from the text of *The Burren, a map of the uplands of North West Clare, Éire,* 1977. This is just one of many wonderful maps and texts of the west of Ireland created by Tim Robinson, Folding Landscapes, Roundstone, Connemara, Co. Galway, Ireland.

from Translations
Brian Friel

Brian Friel's play "Translations" takes us into a hedge school in Baile Beag, Donegal in August 1833. At the end of Act One, Captain Lancey from England is explaining how and why the Royal Engineers are here making the first Ordnance Survey Maps.....

Act One

LANCEY: I'll say what I have to say, if I may, and as briefly as possible. Do they speak *any* English, Roland.

OWEN: Don't worry. I'll translate.

LANCEY: I see. (*He clears his throat. He speaks as if he were addressing children - a shade too loudly and enunciating excessively.*) You may have seen me - seen me - working in this section - section? - working. We are here - here - in this place - you understand? - to make a map - a map - a map and-

JIMMY: *Nonne Latine loquitur?*

(HUGH *holds up a restraining hand.*)

HUGH: James.

LANCEY: (*To* JIMMY) I do not speak Gaelic, sir. (*He looks at* OWEN.)

OWEN: Carry on.

LANCEY: A map is a representation on paper - a picture - you understand picture? - a paper picture - showing, representing this country - yes? - showing your country in miniature - a scaled drawing on paper of- of - of -

(*Suddenly* DOALTY *sniggers. Then* BRIDGET. *Then* SARAH. OWEN *leaps in quickly.*)

OWEN: It might be better if you *assume* they understand you -

LANCEY: Yes?

OWEN: And I'll translate as you go along.

LANCEY: I see. Yes. Very well. Perhaps you're right. Well. What we are doing is this. (*He looks at* OWEN. OWEN *nods reassuringly.*) His Majesty's government has ordered the first ever comprehensive survey of this entire country - a general triangulation which will embrace detailed hydrographic and topographic information and which will be executed to a scale of six inches to the English mile.

HUGH: (*Pouring a drink*) Excellent - excellent.
(LANCEY *looks at* OWEN.)

OWEN: A new map is being made of the whole country.
(LANCEY *looks to* OWEN: *Is that all?* OWEN *smiles reassuringly and indicates to proceed.*)

LANCEY: This enormous task has been embarked on so that the military authorities will be equipped with up to date and accurate information on every corner of this part of the Empire.

OWEN: The job is being done by soldiers because they are skilled in this work.

LANCEY: And also so that the entire basis of land valuation can be reassessed for purposes of more equitable taxation.

OWEN: This new map will take the place of the estate-agent's map so that from now on you will know exactly what is yours in law.

LANCEY: In conclusion I wish to quote two brief extracts from the white paper which is our governing charter: (*Reads*) 'All former surveys of Ireland originated in forfeiture and violent transfer of property; the present survey has for its object the relief which can be afforded to the proprietors and occupiers of land from unequal taxation.'

OWEN: The captain hopes that the public will cooperate with the sappers and that the new map will mean that taxes are reduced.....

MANUS: What sort of a translation was that, Owen?

OWEN: Did I make a mess of it?

MANUS: You weren't saying what Lancey was saying!

OWEN: 'Uncertainty in meaning is incipient poetry' - who said that?

MANUS: There was nothing uncertain about what Lancey said: it's a bloody military operation, Owen! And what's Yolland's function? What's 'incorrect' about the place-names we have here?

OWEN: Nothing at all. They're just going to be standardised.

MANUS: You mean changed into English?

OWEN: Where there's ambiguity, they'll be Anglicised.

MANUS: And they call you Roland! They both call you Roland!

OWEN: Shhhhh. Isn't it ridiculous? They seemed to get it wrong from the very beginning - or else they can't pronounce Owen.

I was afraid some of you bastards would laugh.
MANUS: Aren't you going to tell them?
OWEN: Yes - yes - soon - soon.
MANUS: But they...
OWEN: Easy, man, easy. Owen - Roland - what the hell. It's only a name. It's the same me, isn't it? Well, isn't it?
MANUS: Indeed it is. It's the same Owen.
OWEN: And the same Manus. And in a way we complement each other. (*He punches* MANUS *lightly, playfully and turns to join the others. As he goes.)*
Alright - who has met whom? Isn't this a job for the go-between?
(MANUS *watches* OWEN *move confidently across the floor, taking* MAIRE *by the hand and introducing her to* YOLLAND.
HUGH *is trying to negotiate the steps.*
JIMMY *is lost in a text.*
DOALTY *and* BRIDGET *are reliving their giggling.*
SARAH *is staring at* MANUS.)

Act Two

SCENE ONE

The sappers have already mapped most of the area. YOLLAND'S *official task, which* OWEN *is now doing, is to take each of the Gaelic names - every hill, stream, rock, even every patch of ground which possessed its own distinctive Irish name - and Anglicise it, either by changing it into its approximate English sound or by translating it into English words. For example, a Gaelic name like Cnoc Ban could become Knockban or - directly translated - Fair Hill. These new standardised names were entered into the Name-Book, and when the new maps appeared they contained all these new Anglicised names.* OWEN'S *official function as translator is to pronounce each name in Irish and then provide the English translation.*

The hot weather continues. It is late afternoon some days later. Stage right: an improvised clothes-line strung between the shafts of the cart and a nail in the wall; on it are some shirts and socks. A large map - one of the new blank maps - is spread out on the floor.

OWEN *is on his hands and knees, consulting it. He is totally engrossed in his task which he pursues with great energy and efficiency.* YOLLAND'S *hesitancy has vanished - he is at home here now. He is sitting on the floor, his long legs stretched out before him, his back resting against a creel, his eyes closed. His mind is elsewhere. One of the reference books - a church registry - lies open on his lap. Around them are various reference books, the Name-Book, a bottle of poteen, some cups etc.*
OWEN *completes an entry in the Name-Book and returns to the map on the floor.*

OWEN: Now. Where have we got to? Yes - the point where that stream enters the sea - that tiny little beach there. George!
YOLLAND: Yes. I'm listening. What do you call it? Say the Irish name again?
OWEN: Bun na hAbhann.
YOLLAND: Again.
OWEN: Bun na hAbhann.
YOLLAND: Bun na hAbhann.
OWEN: That's terrible, George.
YOLLAND: I know. I'm sorry. Say it again.
OWEN: Bun na hAbhann.
YOLLAND: Bun na hAbhann.
OWEN: That's better. Bun is the Irish word for bottom. And Abha means river. So it's literally the mouth of the river.
YOLLAND: Let's leave it alone. There's no English equivalent for a sound like that.
OWEN: What is it called in the church registry?
(*Only now does* YOLLAND *open his eyes.*)
YOLLAND: Let's see ... Banowen.
OWEN: That's wrong. (*Consults text.*) The list of freeholders calls it Owenmore - that's completely wrong: Owenmore's the big river at the west end of the parish. (*Another text.*) And in the grand jury lists it's called - God! - Binhone! - wherever they got that. I suppose we could Anglicize it to Bunowen; but somehow that's neither fish nor flesh.
(YOLLAND *closes his eyes again.*)
YOLLAND: I give up.
OWEN: (*At map*) Back to first principles. What are we trying to do?

YOLLAND: Good question.

OWEN: We are trying to denominate and at the same time describe that tiny area of soggy, rocky, sandy ground where that little stream enters the sea, an area known locally as Bun na hAbhann...

Burnfoot! What about Burnfoot?

YOLLAND: (*Indifferently*) Good, Roland. Burnfoot's good.

OWEN: George, my name isn't...

YOLLAND: B-u-r-n-f-o-o-t?

OWEN: I suppose so. What do you think?

YOLLAND: Yes.

OWEN: Are you happy with that?

YOLLAND: Yes.

OWEN: Burnfoot it is then. (*He makes the entry into the Name-Book.*) Bun na hAbhann - B-u-r-n-

YOLLAND: You're becoming very skilled at this.....

With thanks to Brian Friel and to Faber & Faber for their kind permission to reprint these extracts from *Translations* by Brian Friel, Faber & Faber, 1981.

Mapping Alternative Worlds

Barbara Bender

Introduction

We, in the West, have an historically particular way of looking at the world. This post Renaissance 'Western Gaze' skims the surface; surveys the land from an ego-centred viewpoint; and assumes an active viewer and a passive land. The active viewer is part of 'culture' and is gendered male. The passive land is part of 'nature' and is female. The Western Gaze is also about asserting control.

Think about all the knowledge metaphors that we use and you'll see how the Western Gaze colours much of we say and write. We have 'viewpoints', 'overviews', 'landmarks', 'vantage points' and 'ways of looking'. We 'chart new territories', 'explore', 'penetrate', 'break new ground', 'open up new horizons'. We come up against intellectual 'barriers', and operate on 'frontiers'.

Western maps form part of this Western Gaze, and recently geographers have stressed the brooding pervasive power of western cartography(1). They talk about the way in which Post Renaissance maps cover the surface of the world with an homogenous Cartesian grip and present a bird's eye - **lord's eye** - view of the world; about the way in which these maps register a palimpsest of past activities and are mesmerizing in their apparent exactitude, transparency and scientific neutrality.

These geographers question this transparency and neutrality. Wood, for example, points out that when people talk about the map as 'a transparent window on the world', they often fail to look at the framing - the way in which the window isolates one view at the expense of others. We need to question, not just the exactitude of the map, but exactitude in respect to what, exactitude for whom and by whom.

These geographers situate these maps within historically specific social relations. The invention and refinement of the cartographic equipment that made for more accurate mapping was part-cause/

part-effect of developing mercantile capitalism. It wasn't just an adjunct to exploration, colonisation, or the establishment of property rights, it actually created the conditions for such developments. The increasing reliance on maps goes hand in hand with the emergence of the State and with increasing territoriality, surveillance and control. Harley and Wood elucidate the tricks of suppression, enlargement, projection etc. used to enhance the power of western nations.

These deconstructions of the western map are very important: the power of lines on the map whether in colonial, neo-colonial, or post Cold War nationalist carve-ups are all too hauntingly obvious. But perhaps we need also to recognize that these maps, and the Gaze that lies behind them, are not quite so all encompassing, all powerful. We need to consider some of the interstices, resistances and alternative messages. The claustrophobia induced by the western map and the resistance to it are wonderfully described by Borges in *A Universal History of Infamy:*

In that Empire, the Craft of Cartography attained such Perfection that the Map of a Single province covered the space of an entire City, and the Map of the Empire itself an entire Province. In the course of Time, these Extensive maps were found somehow wanting, and so the College of Cartographers evolved a Map of the Empire that was of the same Scale as the Empire and that coincided with it point for point. Less attentive to the Study of Cartography, succeeding Generations came to judge a map of such Magnitude cumbersome, and, not without Irreverence, they abandoned it to the Rigours of sun and Rain. In the Western Deserts, tattered fragments of the Map are still to be found, Sheltering an occasional Beast or beggar..' (2)

In this paper I focus on local knowledge and resistance, on small subversions - first in western contexts and then in 'contact' situations. If this paper could have been longer I would also have talked about non Western indigenous maps. For indigenous maps are not simply a response to colonial encounters. Everyone, everywhere, practices a combination of person-centred 'practical mastery' which depends upon their activities, perceptions and bodily actions, and object-centred mental mapping in which the position of places is defined 'absolutely'. For many people these maps remain in the mind, but sometimes they also take material form.

Western Maps in Western Contexts

Official maps are part of the panoply of authority. There is control over what is and is not on the map. Nuclear installations and the like can be, and often are, left out. But there is often a tension between such omissions and the desire for *comprehensive* coverage. Moreover, property or landclaims are, by definition, bounded. Bordering the landed estate on an English Ordnance Survey map are the remains of the Common, between the grand boulevards of Paris lies the under-stated (but thereby, if desired, almost more visible) warren of tenements and slums. There are many writers who have insisted on focusing attention on the wrong side of the property boundary - on the significance of the vanishing contours of the commonlands or on the disruption of working class urban districts (3).

There is also the possibility of using the controlling overview of the official map as the starting point for a very different being-in-the-landscape sort of approach. After all, alongside the more pervasive metaphors of control that I noted above, there are others that capture a different, more humble way of being in the world: 'taking a particular path', an intellectual 'cul-de-sac', getting lost, not seeing the wood for the trees, 'taking a first step', being trapped.

These lived-in mapped worlds may be more or less subversive. Walter Benjamin, a German jew who resisted the Nazis, fled to Paris and eventually committed suicide, challenged the whole notion of the western map as a means of orientation and as a compendium of scientific knowledge. Whether in Vienna, or Berlin, or most passionately in Paris, he used the map in order to get lost:

Not to find one's way in a city may well be uninteresting and banal. It requires ignorance - nothing more. But to lose oneself in a city, as one loses oneself in a forest, that calls for quite a different schooling. The signboards and street names, passers-by, roofs, kiosks, or bars must speak to the wanderer like a cracking twig under his feet in the forest...(4)

This is a fine illustration of the system of checks and balances between a subject- and an object-centred world. Benjamin loses himself, and then, through 'practical mastery' finds himself in relation to significant places, names and passers-by.

At other times, Benjamin subverts the authoritative purposes of the official map, refuses the palimpsest of historical event, and imposes his own history of jumbled memories. He collapses personal time into space. He imagines taking 'the general staff's map of a city centre':

I have evolved a system of signs and on the grey background of such maps, they would make a colourful show if I clearly marked in the houses of my friends and girl friends, the assembly halls of various collectives, from the "debating chambers" of the Youth Movement to the gathering places of the Communist youth, the hotel and brothel rooms that I knew for one night ... and the graves that I saw filled.. (5)

At one level this is no more than the isolated biography of an individual, but it is also a map of subversion - the Youth Movement, the gathering place of the Communist youth, the brothel, untimely deaths - plotted/plotting against the General Staff map. These are places and spaces of political and personal resistance, of memory and action. In and of itself this will not bring the State to its knees, (indeed the Nazis brought about Benjamin's own untimely death), but it does suggest, quite brilliantly, not just the interplay between lived experience/ embodied space and the larger political and cultural world, but the potential for subversion.

Part of Benjamin's fantasy of alternative ways of mapping has been put into action in contemporary Britain by organisations such as Common Ground which try to get people to draw their own maps: 'authorizing' *their* versions of the world, the places and paths they know as against the grey anonymity of the official map.

These alternative maps emphasise differentiated worlds of experience. At one level they map the everyday places and encounters through which people are socialised and learn to do what is expected of them. But at another, as we have seen, they also map potential nonconformism, ways of questioning - even undermining - the accepted way of doing things.

Western Maps in Contact Situations

I shall do no more than sketch five contact situations, five ways of responding to the Western map. Some do little more than register suspicion or fear, some question, some subvert.

The people of Santa Clara live in shifting settlements on the braiding river course of the Bajo Urumbamba in eastern Peru (6).

They do not make maps, but they do, in their mind and in speech, create kinscapes - 'maps' of social relationships -, places and traces (old gardens, old house-sites) that bind people vis-a-vis each other and the land. It is the older people who tell stories that, as in Benjamin's map and in many of the case-studies that follow, are 'memory work', where time collapses into space.

There is also, however, an *official* map - the land title map created by Government bureaucrats in Lima. This map is very empty. It simply has the boundary lines and coordinates. It takes no account of the shifting nature of the river or the settlements. The map shows that Santa Clara now lies outside the community territory.

This abstract Western map is part of an alien world that is, by and large, irrelevant to the people of Santa Clara. But it is perceived as powerful, and the power is context specific. In a local context, it may, with caution, empower. On very rare occasions the local map has been used to successfully stave off encroachment by the neighbouring white plantation-owner. On the other hand, the copy in Lima has never been used - any attempt to refer matters to the capital is seen as inherently dangerous, for local people perceive that State intervention rarely works to their advantage. In the larger Peruvian political arena, the map is more likely to dispossess than empower.

My second case study is a curious one. In Lahore, Pakistan, there are, of course, official maps, mainly dating back to the British occupation. Local people, however, have constructed, not on paper but in the form of stories and legends, a different map. One that represents an underground world of tunnels that link the gardens, shrines and forts built by the Mughal princes who governed the area over two hundred and fifty years ago. Stories tell of an Imperial tunnel that links Lahore to Delhi, and of provincial tunnels connecting Lahore with smaller places to the West. They speak of armies, several men abreast, marching swiftly along the tunnels (far more swiftly, they say, than on the roads of today!), of modest women moving without harassment, of lovers on secret assignations, of princes cunningly escaping from besieged fortresses. The tunnels are also, especially when associated with rivers, places of danger where demons lurk.

During the Mughal period Lahore had been the provincial capital and even briefly, in the sixteenth century, the Imperial capital. In the eighteenth century it suffered a series of invasions and the Mughal monuments were reduced to ruins. With the British annexation of the mid nineteenth century, new roads, canals and railways further disrupted the old settlement pattern. Thus the Mughal routeways have largely disappeared. And yet the tunnels approximate to likely Mughal roadways. But the tunnels are not real. They exist only in people's imagination.

It seems that the tunnel stories began to circulate in the mid seventeenth century, as the power of Lahore waned. Over time the stories changed and only places that are still visible today are included. The asymmetry between stories told at important Mughal centres and those from lesser sites seems to reflect the original unequal power relations between the centre and the margins. It has been suggested that the tunnel stories represent a genre of popular criticism. 'Things that were (and still are) impossible on the surface, can take place underground' (7). It is a muted form of criticism - no material empowerment, but some psychological advantage.

The third case-study is somewhat more confrontational. The Peruvian government, in the 1970s and 80s wanted to create a nature reserve at Lake Titicaca. It would have involved the control of reed beds that had been owned and used by the local peasant communities for centuries (8). State bureaucrats drew a series of maps which played down the number and location of lake-side settlements, emphasised the island settlements that were to become tourist attractions, and omitted an area of contention. The focus was, as usual, on boundaries and administrative organisation. A sequence of official maps charted the progress of the development.

The peasants also drew maps in order to put their case to the bureaucrats. They used the same approximate orientation, same distinction of land and water. They appended names to settlement locations. But their maps were not to scale, did not include towns, and exaggerated the proximity of settlements. Their maps moved between the conventional over-view and a ground view: houses and mountains were shown vertically. The maps, faithful to indigenous perceptions, showed the natural features cradling the settlements. Each settlement was crowned with a small Peruvian flag - co-opting the official insignia of power.

The bureaucrats and the peasants talked past each other. The bureaucratic maps were primarily for consumption by other bureaucrats, the peasants' maps were mulled over within their own communities. The maps were exchanged, but neither side 'saw' the other's map. For the bureaucrats the peasants' maps were mere sketches. Nonetheless, though based on different conceptions - or misconceptions -, the peasants had done as asked, they had provided 'documentation', and perhaps their maps had some effect. At any-rate, the bureaucrats did not put their plans into action, and the peasants were able to continue to cull their reed beds.

In the final case-studies - one from Papua New Guinea, the other, Australia - the resistance is more overt.

When, in 1885, the Germans colonised New Ireland, off the northeast coast of Papua New Guinea, they broke up the indigenous Malangan settlements and territories and moved the population down to plantations on the coast (9). The indigenous people then began to make very fine three dimensional wooden funerary sculptures. The Germans assumed that they were traditional funerary markers, analogous to grave-stones. They admired them greatly, encouraged their production, bought them, and put them in museums. They entirely failed to understand that these 'traditional' pieces were in fact three dimensional 'maps' - part of the dynamic of land appropriation and transmission. They thus unwittingly encouraged the subversion of their own mapped universe of political boundaries and property relations.

In the making of Malangan sculptures it is the process rather than the end product that is important - the making of the sculpture at the death of an existing holder, the brief display and the competition to win the rights to reproduce the Malangan sculpture. The destruction of the sculptures is important, because it allows a re-creation the next time round. When an anthropologist tried to map, in conventional Western terms, the settlements and pathways, she was told she was wasting her time. The settlements and pathways would change:

After every mortuary ceremony which witnesses sculptural production and the re-allocation of land, the surface appearance of the land is restructured according to a map laid down in memory... (10)

If Kuchler *had* made the map, she would have defined 'permanence' where the Malangans recognized transience and changeability, she would have created precisely the sort of powerful representation that the German occupiers desired, one of fixed boundaries, a record of land-ownership and of social relations *imposed upon* a landscape rather than *implicated in* the landscape. As it was, she saw something that the Germans had failed to see - a way of mapping that permitted continuity in the face of colonisation and fragmentation.

My final example of resistance concerns Australian Aboriginal land-claims. Here I am not concerned with their indigenous maps but with their attempts to work against the grain of the western map.

Western colonisers did not recognize the Aboriginal occupation of Australia, although, on occasion, their placenames acknowledge bloody and unequal encounters. For them, Australia was *terra incognita*, an empty land. Slowly the map filled with the history of white exploration, domination and settlement. Large tracts of new territory were given grandiose names that suggested they were extensions of Europe; mountains and rivers were named after explorers; place-names recorded settlers and their activities. The Aboriginal people, herded onto mission stations or ranches, went unrecorded, though their presence shadowed the white people's place names (11).

In recent years, as Aboriginal people begin to press their land claims, the Western map both inhibits and, to some extent, helps their activities. The White map contains places and lines of communication and boundaries. The Aboriginal people, with a quite different notion of territory, cannot draw equivalent boundary lines. Moreover, the Land Claim bureaucrats recognize only sacred places, not sacred songlines. The continent-wide network of ancestral pathways that connect the sacred sites is, quite literally, ruled out of court. On the other hand, Government acceptance of the significance of sacred sites has had unforeseen consequences. Aboriginal sacred sites are associated with places where people die. Children inherit death names, and the Government accepts that Aboriginal named inheritance constitutes a claim on the land. But then, wonderful irony, it turns out that because of the forced movement of Aboriginal people to the missions and ranches, the *greatest* concentration of Aboriginal sacred sites is precisely around these 'white' places (12). And so, after all, the unrecorded shadows at the white ranches do have indigenous names, and alternative and increasingly powerful maps are being created.

The (so far, limited) Aboriginal successes are worth celebrating. But there is a price to pay for turning the colonisers' maps back on themselves. The fight is on White terrain, uses White terms, White conventions. Many of the ways through which Aboriginals understand their relationship to the land go unacknowledged; information has to be provided that was once sacred and not publicly available; knowledge that was gender- or age-specific loses its specificity.

But then again, and here we circle back to Benjamin and his staff officers' map, more and more Aboriginal groups have requisitioned the Western Ordnance Survey map *entirely for their own purposes.* They use them to create their own cultural maps. The people of Kowanyama on the Cape York Peninsula of Far North Queensland use a GPS device to locate:

the Dreaming tracks, the stories, the poison places and who belonged where... Environmental and historical information - bush lore, traditional land uses, massacres, meeting places and such like. The result [is] a precise European-style map containing wholly Aboriginal information about the country (13).

Conclusions

These are local knowledges - often, but not always, forged in hostile encounters. Forged but not entirely dependent upon i.e. they also have a life of their own. They are, to use a word I've avoided so far, **indexical**: they're 'indexed' on people's sense of their own history, their own social relationships.

The western map is equally indexical, but pretends not to be. As Turnbull puts it:

In the western tradition the way to imbue a claim with authority is to attempt to eradicate all signs of its local, contingent, social and individual production.(14)

In the western map, history is recorded. But it is over and done with. In many of these alternative maps history is present and future. Benjamin regarded everything he chose to recall of his past as **prophetic** of the future because memory collapses time. The Cumbales of Colombia envision history as **in front** of the observer and as **working back** from the observer. It is in front because they **live the consequences today and can change them.**

That, optimistically, could be the message of the maps. The western map is the reality, the technology, the metaphor of global capital penetration. The alternative maps are equally the reality, technology and metaphor of local resistance. The results are as variable as the people and situations involved.

References

1. Harley, J.B. Maps, knowledge and power. In Cosgrove D. & Daniels S. (eds) *The Iconography of Landscape***,** Cambridge University Press, 1988; Harley, J.B. Deconstructing the map. In Barnes T.J. & Duncan J.S. (eds) *Writing Worlds. Discourse, Text and Metaphor in the Representation of Landscape*, Routledge, 1992; Turnbull, D. *Maps are Territories. Science is an Atlas,* University of Chicago Press, 1989; Wood, D. *The Power of Maps,* Routledge, 1993.

2. Borges, J.L. *A Universal History of Infamy,* Transl. N T di Giovanni, p. 131, Penguin, 1975.

3. Edholm, F. The view from below: Paris in the 1880. In Bender B. (ed) *Landscape: Politics and Perspectives,* Berg, 1993; Hammond, J. L. & B. *The Village Labourer,* Guild Books, 1948; Davis, M. *City of Quartz,* Verso, 1990.

4. Benjamin, W. *One Way Street and Other Writings,* Verso, 1985.

5. Ibid .

6. Gow, P. Land, People and Paper in Western Amazonia. In Hirsch E. & O'Hanlon M. (eds) *The Anthropology of Landscape,* Clarendon Press, 1995.

7. Wescoat, J.L. Brand M. & Mir N. Gardens, roads and legendary tunnels: the underground memory of Mughal Lahore. *Journal of Historical Geography* 17, 1, 1-17, 1991

8. Orlove, B. S. Mapping reeds and reading maps. *American Ethnologist* 18, 3-38, 1991.

10. Kuchler, S. Landscape as memory: the mapping of process and its representation in a Melanesian society. In Bender B. (ed) *Landscape: Politics and Perspectives,* Berg, 1993.

11. Ibid.

12. Morphy, H. Colonialism, history and the construction of place: the politics of landscape in northern Australia. In Bender B. (ed) *Landscape: Politics and Perspectives*, Berg, 1993; Strang, V. *Uncommon Ground. Concepts of Landscape and Human-Environmental Relations in Far North Queensland.* D.Phil thesis, University of Oxford, 1994.

13. Morphy, as above.

14. Strang, as above.

15. Turnbull, as above

Barbara Bender is Reader in Material Culture, Department of Anthropology, University College, London.

A longer version of this paper will appear in a book on landscape edited by P Ucko and B Layton in the One World Archaeology Series published by Unwin Hyman.

Making Sense of our Place: a critical review of Parish Maps

David Crouch

Introduction

From the start, the Parish Maps project aimed to do gentle things: '*to encourage communities to chart the familiar things which they value in their own surroundings, and give active expression to their affection for the everyday and commonplace whether in town or country*'. (Common Ground 1987)

There is an important gentleness in the way we may come to 'hold' places we know well, love, care for. However, these gentle words contain much more. They amount to a radical and pioneering claim to the way people make sense of where they live. More than that, they are about making claims on places. Places can symbolise no less than where we are in the world. Contemporary lives are diverse, and sometimes the Parish Map may be taken to read an assumption of something old, of continuity, holding on, when the people doing the Map may be new arrivals. What difference, if any, does this make to ways in which we not only make sense of where we are, but in terms of claims we may make on that place?. What we read from the Map matters; as does what we communicate through the Map, to people familiar with the place, and those who are not.

Parish Maps are, then, very English vehicles for sensitivity and for action. They celebrate attachment. They can be used to steady the view, and the pulse, in local disagreements; their 'beauty' and pleasing prospect can overide the embedded tensions amongst the people in a place. Their singularity can conceal a deeper diversity.

Place itself is intricately bound in much more than a surface geography. That geography includes memory, often collective memory; actions, relationships, happenings, numerous and complex values and facts that are more to do with people than place; feelings than surface. Places today are as complex as contemporary lives; many people live in one place, but events in their lives occur elsewhere. Moreover, their social relationships may stretch widely, globally; the memory that is inscribed upon the place where they live and that gives it such value, positive or negative, may be brought in from somewhere else, sometimes just from our imagination.

People today, as ever, do not all feel a positive association and meaning invested in place; the meaning they hold may be negative. It is perhaps these kinds of place that most concern Common Ground and seekers after common ground. Common Ground's vigour came from a realisation of the elitism in official Conservation; perhaps the next stage is to attend to stimulating reflection, perhaps action, amongst people who may have neutral, or negative images of where they are. We explore this rich if sometimes uneven range of what Parish Maps are, and make an effort to restate some of these facets in this essay, and do so with the help of eight maps.....

Some key themes

Parish

There is a problem, as well as a rich fertility, with the name Parish. Richard Mabey was aware of this early on *'Parish' is a value laden concept* (nothing wrong with that - author).... *ecclesiastical administration,... history, ...loyalties.* (Mabey 1980).

But how can Parish Maps overcome the traditionalist, conservative, perhaps inhibiting potential they hold? Moreover, many places don't find Parish a label they identify with; in cities; amongst people who are not moved by the ecclesiastical historical feel of the word. However, without a tradition of The Parish, places in Scotland have made Parish Maps, Wales has developed the same idea (via the Countryside Council for Wales) with the title The Local Jigsaw/y Jigso Lleol, which is perhaps a direction for relabelling Parish Maps. Although Parish has a strong meaning that is to do with local democracy, this dimension has perhaps suffered in the popular imagination in respect of the more conservative image it has acquired in recent history.

maps and pictures; method and process

Parish Maps are only one of many means that Common Ground has used and developed. They are both maps and pictures. It does appear that Parish Maps offer a particularly good chance for reflection on what matters; for reflection amongst a group of people, and a means of reflecting in such a way that can be enjoyed, and communicated. The very process of making and communicating - in the making, and in the end product - is itself important. However, the making of maps and pictures are both charged with inhibition for many people, and this is an issue to address if a new wave of maps is likely to happen.

knowledge
Parish Maps may be cuddly in their intimacy; friendly, warm; something you feel you can hold, and hold onto. But they offer the chance for much more than that. They can represent nothing less than a focus around which to make claims to contest power over our lives; even if as power extended over features of the physical world around us. Yet often what sounds simply that, can mean very much more. Parish Maps teach officials who claim accuracy in environmental measuring that they frequently misunderstand what actually matters in peoples' lives. Geographical knowledge: a very distinctive way of knowing.

These facets are all about knowledge, a geographical knowledge where place features, people's activities, relationships, sites, memories, are embodied in our trace of the place. This is making geographical knowledge; not in the academy, but 'out there', where we live and work; make values outside the marketplace. These result from looking, moving, feeling, shifting, staying, engagement, remembering, hoping, making friends, doing things together.

roots
Knowing a place has to do with numerous dimensions, as we have seen. Those dimensions can be about rootedness, (re)discovering that memory, celebrating a warmth grounded in activities, practice, doing things with people you know. In a mobile shifting society such as ours, it may be difficult to assert such a 'situated' claim; it may be more one of drawing together a series of rather diverse threads, which may become more of a kaleidoscope than a frameable 'old master'. This points to the importance of knowledge, and the openess to knowledge, knowledge that varies amongst as many people as live in a place. They are about a very distinctive geographical knowledge.

to celebrate, contest, protect
It is for this reason that we are talking about much more than 'sense of place': that sense is about the visual, but also about the way we come

to know a place; about love and care, but also about human relationships, opposition, power and a claim to ownership - not as legal, or financial, but a much bigger sense of ownership that is feeling a place is your own because it includes, embraces fragments, meanings that you feel are your own life.

In this, we are alert to the essentially contradictory poetics of place. People may make maps to make claims, locally, borne of friendship and shared experience (which may deserve 'community'), but also through one dimensional reaction, elitism. People may get together to make a Map from their memory, relationships and experience; or to reach an imagined image of a place, more like an estate agent's dream than a place where ordinary people can still enjoy their own patch. There is nothing inevitably exclusive about this, but there might be something more friendly and inclusive than protecting one's investment.

making pictures

There is a particular aesthetic problem here. The popular way of imagining a Map is to meet certain 'official' requirements - scale, proportion; order across the page; clarity of being read, perhaps portability, and so on. When this is extended to a Map to be framed, this imposes further stress on our intention, with Common Ground, of being something to which we feel attached; of feeling we know our map and that map is ours. It can become loaded with the popular idea of an Old Picture; 'properly' produced, without which it would have no sense of Pride; proud place, proud map, proud people.

One possible limitation on what Parish Maps can achieve is contained in these very ideas that there is one way of doing a map, that it must conform to clearly, perhaps narrowly, proscribed construction, design and presentation. This can suggest a school-learnt procedure, that can inhibit, if you don't feel you can make the standards. This can stifle exactly what Common Ground sought to achieve, in content and style. That is to liberate people to (re)discover what is NOT formally, officially, regarded as proper information, presented with a required accuracy of measurement, mapping ability. It is important that people who may make a Parish Map do not feel constrained by these chains of 'the official' and 'the Proper'. Otherwise, we will discover the repetition of the Town Plan and all its criteria; the Tourist Guide; what is Worthy, and so on. We may need to ignore what is Worthy, to rediscover the oft unsung, unofficial, parts of the world we value.

Painting can wonderfully liberate people's feelings, and give voice to expression freely. Yet for some of us it can be an inhibition. In painting, we discover that the tendency is to apply formal methods of representation, with little adjustment; to do so makes us secure, and when you are challenging official views, it can be felt to need security as a platform. Ironically, it is in the commissioned artists' work that we find not elitism, rule-sticking and Proper work, but freedom; a sense of having permission to connect with what is felt really to be valued. We discover that 'aesthetics' is something that is relative, not absolute; grounded in social mores and culture, not to be dictated.

Resume

It is fascinating to compare two key planks of Common Ground's Project on Parish Maps to encourage everybody to make a Map; and to stimulate this by what are called 'exemplars'. These are sometimes whacky and off the wall ideas of what *can* be done in the way of liberating what makes us value places we know. This can mean tracking the geographical knowledge of place; discovering how our lives and the place where at least part of those lives are spent interact in our knowledge. This comparison, as we observe later in this essay is instructive, and often surprising.

Over two thousand Parish Maps have been made already amongst some the ten thousand villages and towns and cities in the UK since 1987. This is a phenomenal achievement. This has had no central government programme, no recognised commercial potential, but done. Does this represent a flowering of human potential, and anarchic muddle, or one theme copied a thousand times? There is value in each of these, and help and ideas from someone else usually assists. The materials alone are a source of amazement: although many Maps are produced on paper or board, a few feet each way in dimensions, some lean to more sculptural and textile making: video, tapestry, collage, ceramic.

Many different people have become involved; some maps are produced by one individual, an autobiography of a place; in others, every resident has been given a questionnaire to solicit views and values, sometimes businesses too; in several counties, including Cambridgeshire, Cheshire, Devon and Staffordshire, the Women's Institute has been foremost in stimulating their members to make a Map. Although Common Ground never intended a formula, or Officials to organise anyone to do a Map, some stimulation has proven helpful, and not necessarily a strait-jacket: in Devon, the Planning Department has been very active in this way; in Cheshire the Landscape Trust. In Shropshire, the arts officer of the Rural Community Council has been at the forefront of publicising the Common Ground idea locally. In some places, as in Charlbury, Oxon, which we consider below, the local organiser of the Map read about the idea in 'The Times'. It is this very diversity that Common Ground sought, with welcomingly rich diversity in results.

One key curiosity for us must be to discover to what extent Maps have underlined an existing point of view and group already articulate, or brought new perspectives, engaged a new population, unfamiliar to being given a voice; new angles on what matters; new meanings to everyday features.

Four examples from the everyday

The more familiar version of the Map is exemplified, with good result, in Charlbury, Oxfordshire. The Map is a rectangle, on paper, with a plan of the place in the centre, and a border filled with cameos, fragments of life and buildings in the village - chess club, sport, choir, children, meals on wheels and the library, buildings, represented in drawings. This is selective, and omits, for example, a local 1960's school, now a Community Centre widely used. This is a Map for accuracy: OS base, footpaths meticulously marked (the makers sought a show of the footpaths to defend their loss), factual inscriptions written on the Map, layout of streets, fields and hills beyond; carefully painted, in watercolour. I know Charlbury intimately, my parents lived there for seven years; this Map captures much of the place.

Away from the softer South, Lockwood hangs on the north side of the north Yorkshire Moors, and made a very different kind of Map. A large collage nine feet square, its thick material represents the surface of moor, children's playground, a terrace of houses and a spoilheap, symbolic of the working history of the place. This Map took the exercise to the limit and worked the draft of ideas round every hamlet in a scattered Parish, to fairs, meetings and fetes, where everyone was invited to spend a while in discussion, arguing over what mattered.

Standlake is another village in Oxfordshire. It presents a very different 'face'. Seventy square sketches frame the central street layout. The layout is sketched in, and the seventy small images are each drawn by a different person/ group and depict things in everyday life as varied as the view from a child's bedroom window, a NO sign to a local gravel company, capturing the warmth and excitement of place, as well as the contesting of the place's 'soul'. This makes a kaleidoscope with an uneven border, a real effort to impart the diversity of everyday life and both blue remembered hills and real local conflicts, where claims need to be felt and made.

Another variegated version is in the (sub)urban district of Westbury Park, in Bristol. As much words as pictures and photographs, and childrens' sketches, this is a celebration of diversity: 'Chinese shop for when the freezer is empty', and 'step into wilderness allotments'; 'Westbury Green; slip in doggy do'. There is a sense of unabashed everyday life here, where no rules have been used to sift the material. It is arranged as a Monopoly Board, and was the almost 'instant' result of request for material at a local fete.

Five very Artistic examples

Simon Lewty has 'always been fascinated by land and geography; how we connect what we know of the place with what is already there' (in conversation, 1994). His Parish Map touches the surface at every millimetre; but it goes deep too. The shapes, colours and textures of his Map are made with words which represent feelings, memories, myth and the step of a local walk, by hedges and feeling the wind: 'merging in the imagination with a fragmentary mental landscape, whose paths are like fissures in the earth, constantly opening onto new levels of interpretation' (Lewty quoted in Sinden and Clifford 1987).

Like making a trace in the ground, The Map by David Nash gets in touch with the physical in our own bodies, always in touch with the ground 'the boundary of my personal Parish, a form of extended physical body, the area within which I feel in direct contact with a sense of home'. Here is a sense of being and belonging, not necessarily writ in buildings or other props, adequately a sense of earth. Another way into a place is knowing features that remind, most often, of human encounters, people with whom that place is shared. Balraj Khanna, whose colliding human encounters centre the universe on Lord's cricket ground offer an open, plastic form and buzz: a Universe in one place.

But life, and place, are not always happy go lucky. Steve Willatts has, for some years, worked with young people making maps of where they live, in forgotten parts of the city while Conrad Atkinson has long campaigned for change in the way people's homes are exploited by somebody else. Willatts' photomontage captures a village's worth of people living in a tower block (whose 'own place' might be the rough vacant ground round the corner, Home, escape and their identity). Atkinson's words overpower the map - strontium, caesium, plutonium, leukaemia - reminding us of the hazards of everyday living in a small town the wrong side of the Lake District. Concerns like this can be more important than wanting to make celebration, and the Map provides a powerful tool to articulate this.

Review

unity and diversity

Parish Maps, like any Map, must include and omit. There is a process of selectivity which is partly 'artistic', partly social, partly political; avoiding offence, or making a point. Selecting out buildings used by everyone, because they are not in the olde worlde image of a village raises questions about what in everyday life is 'on show'; whose and why; to whom. A process of filtering is more difficult when more people are involved, and that means debate: making the map becomes part of the village getting to know itself. Looking like a'family photograph' may be appealing, and this is understandably made to us. Yet omitting members of the family, or hiding real issues may keep those family difficulties stewing - which is perhaps harder to do when there are real issues over the future of the place; real matters of inclusion and exclusion amongst the 'community'. There can be a case for making a Map as a kaleidoscope of fragments, even four or more different Map panels, rather than one unitary Map assuming total representativeness and inclusion.

content and articulation

Although all four Community Maps noted here were enjoyed, celebrated life, and make wonderful images, most have an edge that is telling a present day story also to influence someone else. These included fighting a gravel pit extension, safeguarding footpaths, turning round a Parish declined from ironstone working to confidence amongst the people who live there, and with an outward message for tourists in industrial heritage.

boundaries and edges

Although the people making these Maps felt the place to hold an important sense of 'turf', of ownership (not in any legalistic, or financial sense), they also draw attention to its linkages with what is otherwise an obscured 'outside world'. Hard lines around the edge, a white nothingness beyond, suggest security, but that can be mixed with claustrophobia. In one of our Maps, an image of a train hurtling out of the picture 'to London' connects these different worlds in which many live today, and demonstrate too that we are not dependent on a 'global' business community, but are semi-detached from it and to it, with our own identity, often together, often overlooked.

parish, home, community.

The Map is not an end in itself; it is a step along a journey, which is a personal and collective journey in the place. This familiarly contains collective memory, as many of the things people do in a place are shared; bingo, walking the dog and meeting neighbours, as well as solitary; a history through which what matters today was produced. Where many people have been involved, and the Map produced over perhaps years, more chance emerges for the making of the Map, the process itself, to influence a wider scan of events, ideas and decisions. Many Maps we have looked at seem to stop at yesterday, or a century ago, as though nothing mattered since the Big House was built. Other Maps celebrate the coming to an end of a period of time - a centenary. Of course, that can be enormously informing if it is seen as a bus stop on the way to another stage in its life, with a chance to use the Map as a marker and to relate actions and feelings and influences into the future. If the content of the Map is about today, and aspirations for tomorrow, more potential exists for highlighting everybody's interest, the more potential there is for influencing debate beyond the place itself, and officials.

maps and pictures

When these maps are finished, they often appear on the wall of the local hall, where most people have a real chance to see it. It becomes a spectacle, an icon of what the place is about, what makes it tick and how it does so. The Map becomes an Exhibition. But it is also there to be a part of a continuing life of that place. It can be rendered static, a celebrated past. The chance it is given to influence awareness, ideas and claims will mean that the Map has more of an ongoing value in the continuing life of the people and its place. Some Maps have been changed, negotiated as people looking have suggested additions. That way, the Map is taken from being an Oil Painting of what was at a moment in time, proscribed by a few, perhaps, to being an influence that continues in the life of the people around it.

art and identity

The difference between expected and received 'good aesthetics' and what contemporary professional painters do is instructive. In many of the paintings there is a welcome celebration of local interest, local clubs and societies; rocks, pillars, hedgerows with a memory of the planter, local legends and memories that make the place, and people's felt lives, distinctive, and meaningfully 'theirs'. Yet there are many maps, even with these features, where the reading comes through as a constraint on what should be shown; an effort to make it look 'right'; to formalise, overselect. Without doubt all of these maps made are a joy, and an informer to people's lives, but sometimes they might work to a formula that takes the exercise back again into those Official regulations and expectations that Common Ground and hundreds of the Maps have sought to wriggle from. It is sometimes the contemporary artists who have succeeded, perhaps better able to rework, or 'play' with their medium; perhaps seeking a less conservative, more radically liberating, progressive result. In any case, what is 'right', what is considered 'aesthetic' is at least partly a social thing; the rules, the academy. But in Parish Maps, we seek that knowledge outside, beyond someone else's limits. The Parish Map is 'ours'.

summary and possibilities

In making the Map, we discover the material, physical, architectural and also the very sensuous, and about feelings and hopes; the metaphorical, the stories and the evocation of memory shared. The place turns out to be as much people, in most cases, as it is inert physical features; the challenge to power and the claims for ownership. Although sometimes singularly autobiographical these are more frequently shared autobiographies, which is where the notion of community comes close.

building community and the process of making a Map;
Parish Maps don't make community, but the process of putting together a Map offers the opportunity of engagement; of meeting, sharing, getting deeper into what matters about a place. This can go beyond simply recounting landmarks, to realisations of why they matter. This means using the process to explore, needing time, and not a closed agenda.

empowerment
Parish Maps can have progressive, or regressive, potential, too. They can silence diversity, or empower. In making that Map, we discover that different people know, and value a place in different ways, and come to understand that value through different pathways. This means for anyone making a Map, to talk in languages that different groups will comprehend, not because of any hierarchy of knowledge, but difference. Some people know places through abstracts of 'architecture', 'local information', symbols that attracted them here. Others know the same place more through a patina of personal relationships, memories of people and events, so the meanings are about people, and talking 'place' misses the point. If Parish Maps are to fulfill a really progressive potential, it is imperative that they reach all those parts of the social life that regular, recognised measurement does not understand, in the way it is meaningful to people there. Issues unsuspected at the start of the process may emerge.

making positive
Perhaps the greatest challenge to Mapping is to turn its vigour to places that have only neutral, even negative meanings for people who know them. Many places have been awarded negative images over the years, as other places are formally 'labelled'. People living in many places have not held on to a sense of heritage, omitted from formal labels and listing. This may require discovering the ways in which places, as people their lives in that place, are valid and valued, in a way that does not need official recognition.

Moreover, Parish Maps have only slowly made headway in towns and cities. There are big exceptions, such as Avon/ Bristol, Sheffield and Sunderland. The word 'Parish' did not hinder these. Going further will be assisted by financial support from the Urban Regeneration Project to complement the excellent support from the Countryside Commission and Rural Action.

everyday life
Finally, Parish Maps are not only about ordinary places; they are about everyday life. Everyday life has been treated as downbeat, by High Culture and Popular Culture alike. Attending to the every day is most likely to add personality, not 'personalising' to the 'ever-same' of much contemporary culture. Knowledge of geography is embedded in everyday actions, interactions, memory, and owes only part to the media, tourism images, and commercialised promotion, from which our actual knowledge is semi detached. Many people can add to Official knowledge.

knowing our place
Like songs, Maps are at their richest when people working them are inspired by their own lives, making their own rules, only faintly observing what somebody else somewhere else has done. Equally, the best Maps are not parochial, but engage the complex, varied and changing identities of the mix of people that make up place; produced through a dialogue not always happy and equal, of place, people, other places and other people that inform us. The combination of outward vision and local intimacy is the source of this inclusive richness. One of the people who made one of the Parish Maps reviewed in this essay put it this way:
it was intended as something to celebrate the opening of the new village hall; but in the process we discovered a real concern for the extension of the gravel workings proposed near the village, and the Map soon developed into a means for the whole village to express concern over this.

Another:
People discovered through doing the Parish Map a way forward for the future of the place: It has proved not to be an end in itself, but a step along the way.

Of course, people have multiple and diverse loyalties, and to burden a Parish Map with bringing all this together is too much, but it helps. To do just a Map and bring in all the enjoyment as well as enthusiasm that stimulates may be enough.

We turn to the artist Sheila Fell, not for Design Guidance, but for earthing the sensuality of our knowledge: 'The world is a sum of its parts and the parts are all local. Its news is all local news, as every bit of earth is home to somebody'.

Note:
The discussion on Artists' Maps include observations by David Matless (Crouch and Matless 1996);
Sheila Fell's words are taken from Sheila Fell, South Bank Centre, 1990

Other sources
Common Ground, *'Knowing your place'* exhibition leaflet, 1987
Crouch, D. *The cultural experience of landscape*, Landscape Research 15, 1. 1990
Crouch, D. and Hennessey, N. *Local knowledge; community maps and empowerment,* Ecos 16, 3/4 December 1995
Crouch, D. and Matless, D. *Refiguring Geography; the Parish Maps of Common Ground*,Transactions of the Institute of British Geographers, March 1996
Mabey, R. *The Common Ground*, Hutchinson, 1980
Sinden, N. and Clifford, S. *A map of your own place*, Geographical Magazine, March 1987

David Crouch is the Head of Rural Development and Leisure Research Group at Anglia Polytechnic University.

The Making of the Real Centre of the Universe

Balraj Khanna

The original brief for Common Ground's exhibition "Knowing Your Place" stated that the Parish Map did not have to be about where one lived; that it should be of a place of particular meaning to the artist. It was a generous brief. However, as I thought about it, I felt I wanted my Map to tell a story. Not a conventional one with a beginning, a middle and an end, but a story which would somehow give a glimpse of something very personal to me, involving my past and present. At the same time, I did not want it to be an illustration, for I knew there was no story really, only a view of a relationship with where I once lived as a child and a youth in India, and I where lived at the time of painting this picture, Maida Vale, next door to Lords Cricket Ground.

In 1952 the Indian cricket team came to England on its first post-Independence tour. Not yet twelve then, I was already a serious cricket addict. Like any boy of my age who loved the game, I lived for it - I could have gone to bed with pads and gloves on. Living in a small dusty town in the Punjab, I would remain glued to the radio during most of the five days of the test matches. It was then that I first heard of Lords and what it stood for. I have ever remained bewitched by the magic of the name (passing by it on my first day in this country ten years later, I had held my breath when my friend and host, who lived next door to the building later glorified by one Charles Saatchi, pointed it out to me from the bus).

Thinking retrospectively, although I had no idea whatsoever what my Map was going to look like, one important aspect of it became clear to me as soon as I began making preliminary sketches for it, its title. Artists often agonise over titles of their works which is why so many 20th century paintings are feebly called 'Untitled'. In this case, it came to me in a flash -'The Real Centre of the Universe'.

But the real centre of the universe was not my home in a Maida Vale mews where I lived then and still do today. It was Lords Cricket

Ground where I had watched Sobers and Kanhai delight a packed Lords during my first summer here circa 1963, where I have seen electrifying performances by all-time greats, such as, Dexter, Cowdrey and Boycott, and where I saw Kapil Dev lift the World Cup after beating the invincible West Indies exactly twenty summers later.

With the title came a telescoped view of what I would do, weave the tapestry of the whole area around Lords, which is a stone's throw from my mews. I painted the ground as if I were looking at it seated on a cloud. Aerial photographs show Lords as a large rectangular huddle of covered and uncovered stands with round edges. I took liberties and made it oval, more like a lingam to lend it a certain mystique which a lingam emanates. Also, I made the ground dark, like a lingam, to enhance the effect.

I did not place Lords in the middle of the canvas, which would have made the compostion look contrived. Anyway, you do not 'compose' a map. I wanted it to be an important part of an urban area seething with life, activity and colour. St John's Wood Road in the picture has the yellow and orange of the MCC tie. The rippling Grand Union Canal running parallel to it reminded me of the canals and rivers of my own beloved Punjab. This led me to wonder about something I had never thought of hitherto - that the Punjab (which literally means 'land of five rivers', a name given to it by the ancient Persians) and its numerous canals did not have any boats!

Most bridges in India, large or small, have names. There is the great Howrah Bridge spanning the mighty Hooghly in Calcutta (as the holy Ganges is called in Bengal), or the Such and Such Bridge over a dry trickle on the road to an unheard of village. The bridges in Little Venice, Maida Vale have no names. This inspired me to donate a name to at least one of them, the quaint, cobalt and blue structure that allows leafy Warwick Avenue to flow gracefully into traffic-harassed Harrow Road. Only I am aware of this fascinating fact and the person after whom the bridge is named - Krishna.

Years ago, while walking across this rather attractive example of civil engineering with a rather attractive friend called Krishna, I was moved to relieve the bridge of the burden of anonymity and bestowed her name on it. "I name thee Krishna Bridge ... " I proclaimed grandly.

The friend came and went, but the bridge remains, as does my name for it, albeit only in my memory.

Obviously, there lived in my area at the time of the painting of the Map a graffiti artist with wit. Walls of derelict properties were festooned with spray-can notices with irresistible puns and observations - 'Dwelling Unit','Sweet Dwelling Unit', 'God is a Myth', 'the Earth Sucks', 'Economy is the Police of Sense' and such like. I indulged in some flagrant plagiarism and incorporated a couple of these delectable quotes in my painting without being able to acknowledge my debt to their author, for I knew not his identity.

On a September evening of an Indian Summer, I had received two invitations - first for drinks in Primrose Hill and to dinner later, in Hampstead. Having overstayed at my first port of call, I rushed out of my friend's house to catch a cab. As I stood waiting for one with my back to the dark hump of Primrose Hill, I received a third invitation - from a lady of uncertain age - to savour the delights of the balmy evening in the park for a modest fee. It was an offer I had to refuse. "I must desist, madam," I said and ran. My hosts in Hampstead laughed when they heard the story. In the Map, this episode is recorded as 'Accosted here', or something similar.

I could go on and on, but now I will desist. I would like to add, though, that I deliberately chose the difficult square format for the picture as opposed to a conventional oblong, more suitable for narrative painting. In the latter, the action unfolds horizontally, you read it like a piece of writing. I did not want to be restricted by any such considerations, preferring instead that my imagery move freely on different levels all at once, telling an anecdote here, touching a point there, but by and large, filling up the whole canvas with pictorial interest laced with an ability to make itself audible and arouse curiosity. To echo the Lords of my painting, I enclosed all this in a vast Lingam shape with a rich brown surrounding.

And what do I think of it now? I really don't know except that I enjoyed painting it and that I would like to do another Map one day.

Balraj Khanna is an artist.

Parish Map (Old Milverton) 1986
Some notes in retrospect

Simon Lewty

There was a tarred road at its beginning and another at its end. In between a track ran across open fields, a footpath linking the outskirts of Royal Leamington Spa with the tiny village of Old Milverton. This was the place I chose when I was invited by Common Ground to contribute to the Knowing Your Place exhibition in 1986.

I had known this path since childhood, when much more of the surrounding area was farmland. I must have walked along it hundreds of times. A walk, whatever the age of the walker, may take in not only landmarks such as trees, hedges, gates, ponds and so on, but also the people and animals we meet, the birds, flowers and stones we see, the changes in light, weather and season. It also includes the history of the land on which we walk, whether we are aware of it or not - that a hedge, for instance, might be (as mine was) part of an ancient parish boundary. It means the footprints we leave behind us, and the thoughts we think as we go. The same walk can mean something different each time it is made, so that familiarity may lead not to contempt, but to renewed astonishment, as the known yields up the unknown.

I did not set out to make a topographical image of the area, but to fuse together both outer and inner experiences of the landscape. Drawing and writing became rather like walking, and walking became both discovery and recollection, as the sights and sounds and smells of the place touched off points of memory and association. The walk took on a shape in space and time which was not to be measured in years, or by a watch; and the images of my map followed this shape, as they developed on the paper. But the landscape never ceased to be mysterious, never fully disclosed itself. I hope this does not sound pretentious or 'psychic' - unlike William Blake, I saw no visions - but I was frequently seized by the thought of the many feet that had walked those paths before me. Before the town of Leamington, indeed, when the nearest human habitations were in Old Milverton, a mile or so distant. It was to this village that the path continued, when it 'ran off' my map. Sometimes I picked up tokens of earlier walkers: a broken clay pipe, the sole of an old shoe, pottery sherds with the trailed 'slip' designs characteristic of the seventeenth or eighteenth century. But these were the rare finds; much more common were the ubiquitous fragments of Victorian tableware. It was easy, especially after rain, to spot these gleaming blue and white specks. If you paused to look at them closely you could sometimes see bunches of roses or tiny Chinese pavilions sunk in the red-brown Warwickshire clay.

My map covered two fields, approached by a tunnel-like path leading from a suburban road. This path was enclosed on one side by a high, close-boarded fence, and on the other by a tangle of shrubs marking the boundary of what used to be an old allotment garden, now entirely grown over. A much-mended wooden 'kissing gate' led into the first field. Although it was not large, the sensation always was of emerging into a great space of light and air, after the narrowness and shade of the fenced approach. Both the fields were rough pasture, and sheep and cows were often to be seen there. The land had not been ploughed in modern times, and the ridge and furrow patterns of medieval strip farming could clearly be seen especially when the sun was low. In a corner of the first field stood an old barn, like the kissing gate a marvellously ramshackle assemblage, put together from bits of wood and partly painted, partly rusting corrugated iron, on a framework of roughly hewn tree-trunks. It was, I believe, what is officially called an 'eyesore', but it never did my eyes any harm, and I put it into my map. It had been erected as a shelter for animals, and stood beside a pond, where they often came to drink. Twenty yards or so from it, four posts stood up in the middle of the field - the largest bearing the marks of hinges. A gateless gateway to nowhere . There were no other traces of the fence that might once have been there, but all the evidence suggested that this field had at one time been subdivided into two - or even three - for a ditch ran at right angles to the line of the posts on the other side of the path. A massive oak tree growing in the hedge was a reminder of the great age of this landscape. The second field was much larger and more open. It was sporadically grazed, but not enough to prevent its colonization by scrubby thorn-bushes, some of which grew to a considerable size. Sheep devoured the tender shoots at the bottom, as high as they could reach, while the cattle attended to the upper parts; thus each bush was nibbled in different ways at different times, creating strange shapes. One summer, in a shimmering heat-wave, I saw the field looking like a great garden of crude topiary pagodas and minarets.

All of this, and much more, provided me with material for many pictures over the years since the Parish Map. The village of Old Milverton itself was to prove intensely fruitful, and I feel that I have still not exhausted the possibilities of the whole area. However, in 1988 something happened which everyone who loves a particular landscape must fear. One day, a large signboard appeared at the entrance to the path leading to the first field and on it was written: FOR SALE BY TENDER. 5th AUGUST 1988. THIS PRESTIGIOUS SITE FOR 12 HIGH CLASS RESIDENCES. I felt both angry and numb: it was the end of a little world.

What happened after that may be briefly summarized. The 'tunnel' path and part of the first field, including the barn and the pond, were sold to a local developer, for over a million pounds, according to a report in the local paper. Soon after that the bottom fell out of the property market. The area to be built on was fenced, the barn bulldozed, and a curving tongue of concrete which was to provide the foundation for a road, built out into the field. Then all work ceased for several years, during which time the devastated area filled up with rubbish, and was spectacularly flooded in winter, all the topsoil having been removed during the construction of the road, which sometimes looked like a concrete jetty surrounded by the sea. Whether the developers realized at the time that the land was a catchment area for water draining off all the surrounding fields, I do not know. Extensive drainage would need to be put in. The pond had to be left more or less intact, as it contained, I was told, great crested newts - a protected species - although I myself never saw them. By now it is probably part of someone's back garden, as the whole area has, over the last two years, seen the promised development of luxury houses and bungalows. The second field was ploughed up at the same time, resulting in the loss of the old strip-field patterns, to say nothing of the footpath, which had to be painfully re-trodden through the mud. So in less than three years the whole area of my Parish Map has been changed out of all recognition.

Could anything have been done to stop it all? I have to say I doubt it, given the mania for 'infill' building which then prevailed, the decrease in land necessary for agriculture, the desire of the private landowner to sell and the marginal status of the land itself. I discussed this with a sympathetic planner who showed me a map marking exactly where the green belt around Leamington began. The second of my two fields was in fact 'green' and so, in theory, protected to a certain extent; but for how long? With the buffer of marginal land in the first field gone, does that mean that the second field has now become marginal? The planner seemed uncertain. If so, there would seem to be no way of preventing the green belt area around towns from being steadily eroded, as they become marginal by default.

Could I myself have done anything to save half a marginal field and a collapsing barn? Should I have tried? When I ask myself these difficult questions I get no clear answer, or rather, the answer is both yes and no, the same as the answer to questions as to whether my feelings about that landscape have changed? Or would I do the Parish Map differently now? The moment I set eyes on that signboard, I knew it was already over. The place would never be the same again. If its 'marginality' led to its downfall, I think it was partly that same marginality that fascinated me. Marginality not in the planner's sense, but in some less defined way - an uncertain quality, the feeling of being on the border of somewhere else, a place belonging wholly to neither town nor country, and with a past whose engrained marks lay only just beneath the surface. How could I have got that over to a planning committee, when I scarcely know how to articulate it to myself? The relationship between an artist and the landscapes he adopts as 'his' is necessarily a very private thing, although he can and ought to share the fruits it may bear. To have campaigned as an artist - and probably alone - would, have involved me in dilemmas I could not have coped with and a commitment I could not have sustained. *All* our loved places are potentially under threat, we should value them the more, and be more vigilant on their account. And I say 'we' because I think that the effort has to be a collective one.

Simon Lewty is an artist.

In Wiltshire and Wales
- the making of two maps - 1986 - 1996 -

Jane Whittle

Ten years ago, in 1986, a group of people living in Redlynch, a sprawling place at the western edge of the New Forest, began to make a map of it. That was the Year of the Environment, when Common Ground were in the pilot phase of the Parish Maps Project, and our embroidered chunk of land, like an eiderdown, representing chalk downs, forest, heath, farmland and the lovely Avon valley, began to take shape, It took two years to make, and one more to complete the footpath guide and the Redlynch Book, both of which sold out very quickly. The quilt received considerable publicity and has been exhibited often but, as yet, has not found the permanent, public, local home it needs, if its message is to continue to be meaningful. Perhaps renewed interest aroused by the 10th anniversary celebrations will help it to do so. We hope it will.

Those were years when many places were threatened by new roads, housing estates and the sudden arrival of prosperous town dwellers seeking a new, quieter life-style. Villages suddenly became noisier. Many people felt strongly about conservation issues, although we discovered that the inhabitants of the original hamlets that had spread out to become Redlynch, felt that what they valued most had been lost during the expansion of brick and tarmac between the wars. It was largely the second wave of incomers, hoping to resist the suburbanizing effects of a third wave, who responded to our Parish Map project. A questionnaire, delivered to every home by the milkman, provided good feed-back when we asked "What would you miss most if it disappeared?" The school children produced a lively book which answered that question graphically and we discovered that people were already photographing local wild flowers, recording old ponds and wells, and counting birds. I think the project did increase a sense of identity in a rather scattered community at a time when it felt threatened by more development. As it turned out, recession may have also helped to defer some of those threats, for a while.

Since then a feeling of protection towards the land itself has continued to grow in the public imagination. We have learned more about how we are poisoning the places which support us, and every year some new threat is made public. Perhaps the earth will eventually shrug off its greedy parasites.

In 1989, with all this in mind, I came to live in a part of Wales which has always been a gap in the map, a place that has probably been by-passed, due to its unique geography, ever since it was first inhabited. Certainly little has changed since I began to spend family holidays here thirty years ago. No motorways, no theme parks, no huge housing estates, no Sainsburys or Marks and Spencers; a place where the silence is as solid as the rock, and the roar of the traffic is replaced by the roar of wind and waves. The fields still have names, there are wild goats, wild cats, pole cats and badgers that breed so successfully they have taken to eating chickens, although the Badger Protection Society is loath to believe it. The balance of nature is fairly weighted against us here so we have to take our rightful place in it. The locals are not over keen on tourism and 'conservation' is not a traditional farmer's word, unless it means a grant; they are doing it anyway. Trees that fall down have always been left to rot, producing, by chance, a favourable habitat for many other living things; hedges are laid; muck is scattered. Sheep have to be subsidized, they keep people on the land, and look after it. Work is scarce. House prices rose after the property boom, but many remain on the market for years. However, for those who do manage to survive here, there also remains..."a space in this old land - somewhere to grow, somewhere to be".

So, making a map in such a place was different from making one in the south of England during the Thatcher years. I was a new-comer in Wales, in spite of thirty years as a familiar face, whereas I had lived in Redlynch for twenty years, although, until we made that map, had not taken an active part in the life of the village. Here I was too new to ask intimate questions. 'Privacy' would probably have been the answer to the Redlynch question; the one more likely to be answered might have been, "What would you like to save for your grandchildren?" But, in the end, we decided not to ask it.

When I put up the first poster (in Welsh and in English) inviting people to take part in the second map project, one village shopkeeper said,

"You won't get many to help you to do that, you know. But they'll love it when you've done it!" He was right. Most people here have very little spare time which is not already fully occupied.

This 'Bro', which produces its own monthly newspaper in Welsh, consists of three villages, two hamlets and a small town. The valley is surrounded by high mountains and opens to the sea in the west. Apart from farming and commerce, occupations include education, medicine, outdoor pursuits, local government, the National Park and an army camp. There are a few very small factories, four primary schools and one comprehensive; several choirs and plenty of clubs; one street of shops; a library; a cinema; a number of pubs, churches and chapels; a 12th century Welsh castle; a manor; a private air strip; a quarry; a sewage works; caravans and camp sites; old people's homes, a sports centre and a hospital. Everything you need, plus an exquisitely varied, un-spoilt and un-threatened landscape almost entirely devoted to sheep. English people who came here first on holiday, or for other reasons, have been inclined to end up living here. In the villages, although most of the small shops have gone, Welsh is still the first language; everybody is related to everybody else, or so it seems. When people have lived in the same place for generations, their links with the land and each other could hardly be stronger. The Welsh word 'hiraeth' describes that special sense of longing a Welsh person feels for home, and home is the 'Bro'.

This map was begun by a small group of friends; it gradually expanded to include seventeen women of all ages, three of whom were born here, and one man who sewed the mountain he saw every day while feeding his chickens. There were others who provided materials, transport and encouragement in various ways, as word went round and the project was featured in the local newspaper, radio and TV. None of this publicity was sought; it just happened. The first exploratory walks were led by an environmental lecturer from Aberystwyth University Extra Mural Department, who also provided the posters, aerial photographs and OS maps. He had seen something about the Redlynch Map in an exhibition at Aberystwyth Arts Centre and thought it would be interesting to do a map project with his walking group. He suggested one village; it grew into another large chunk of land, the boundaries of which were, once again suggested by geography rather than history.

We had to have the mountains and the sea, the lake and the narrow gauge railway. So this map is fourteen feet long, four feet wide and three feet high, in four sections; Redlynch is six feet by seven feet and no more than ten inches high, and can be rolled up. Chalk is so different from slate and granite and the movement of glaciers have left their mark on Welsh rock. To obtain these shapes we used layers of polystyrene for the contours instead of soft stuffing, but the surface has been embroidered in the same way, each person getting to know and sewing their own "milltir sgwar", the patch of land they chose to make. It never ceases to amaze me how well all these patches, made by different people of differing skills, responding in individual ways to a variety of places they have explored on foot, fit together to form one landscape. Each person expresses personal feeling from what they are depicting and yet what they create has unity as well as diversity. I don't think it would work so well if it was done by one person. This process worked in Redlynch and in Wales, although the landscapes are so different. We used the same working methods; scaling up maps, sharing a rough colour scheme relating to altitude, and the scrap heaps of old clothes, wools and silks to embroider the surface details. It is, of course, the incredible diversity and variety in nature that produced individuality and character; the same is true for humanity, if only we were more able to accept our differences. Uniformity is another kind of killer.

In Wales, although it was harder to get people to sustain an active part in the research processes and the making of the map, the responses were marvellous when, at last, a mighty joint effort lead to its completion and it went on show for the first time. It continues to produce welcome feed back. People know every inch of the place so well, they love to see it in miniature, understandable form, with field boundaries, footpaths bridges and houses, all there to be discovered, recognised or remembered. This is how it was, here in 1995. What will it be like in a hundred years from now? Everybody relates to that - the idea of preserving a heritage for future generations, and contributing their bits of the past.

Did we wake up the old red dragon for a minute, feed him a few scraps and make him feel better? He has a long memory. Maybe in the south of England things move on, and are forgotten, more quickly.

Happily the Welsh map has been offered a permanent home. It will live in the 9th century church of St Cadfan, next to the oldest inscribed stone in Wales, where everyone can go and see it at any time, celebrate the wonderful places we share, feel proud of them, and continue to look after them.

Jane Whittle is an artist and writer

Uplyme Parish Map

Christine Case

Quite honestly I had never considered the whole parish of Uplyme before. It was a place I took my children to school in, a place I drove through always admiring the trees as I went, but really I took its beauty and character for granted as I think we often do in a place that is familiar. It is not until changes occur that we notice, but so often it is too late. So if nothing else here was a good reason to make a map, something that simply through awareness would jolt people out of lazy complacency, to appreciation of what they have on their doorstep, and then hopefully, preservation of it.

Lexie Sumner had seen a brief television mention about the project and so through her the seed had been planted in Uplyme. She contacted a number of residents throughout the Parish and got us all together in the Village Hall. We looked at the best wall for the map and made a plan as to how information was to be collected about the area. Little red memo books were issued to a number of people who agreed to collect information about their immediate area. This group of people would therefore be 'Scouts', writing down what they themselves felt or knew about the area but also reading and talking to other people and writing down what they observed.

We duplicated a questionnaire asking such questions as, "What would you most miss about the area?", "Where is your favourite place?", etc and this we issued to local schools, shops and post office.

Whilst this network of collecting information was going on I was looking at enlarged O.S. maps of the Parish and trying to decide how the finished map would look. I can remember feeling slightly panicky at this stage, not quite knowing what I was doing and feeling overawed at the project I had taken on. Beyond a vague idea that the 'map' part should be in the middle with some sort of decorative and informative border around the outside, I hadn't a clue what it would look like.

Another meeting at the Village Hall and the return of collected information from the map group and the map began to gel. Suddenly it grew in size, it felt right to have it as big as the wall allowed. With this growth in size came, for me, the realisation that I needed another pair of artistic hands and brought in a friend, Sally Hargraves.

Between us we planned and very conveniently our interests fell into two areas. Sally worked on the central map - I worked on the illustrated border. We agreed we did not want it to look like a coloured O.S. map. It was to have depth and feeling of looking down on the five valleys, joined in the middle, at the village. Because of this we were not going to be concerned with pinpointing every house and lane on the map. Most would be there but some would disappear behind hills.

Sally and I taped together pieces of paper and began to draw the rough draft. O.S. maps although useful reference did not give the 'feel' of the area, so we made journeys to all the far flung corners of the Parish, all the while taking photographs and looking and remembering so that we could record. During that planning stage of getting the map to look right we wished many times for a pair of wings, how much easier it would have been to look down on the Parish as a whole and take one, all encompassing photograph. Life not being like that, we made collages of photographs until the whole area was covered.

My spare room became the map's room. No visitors for 9 months, a 6ft x 5ft lodger instead. Gradually the room also filled with papers, reference books and magazines, tracings, notations, drawings and maps. This map became part of the household, it demanded attention, it excited me, it drained me of energy, in many ways it was like a fourth child. I felt proud of it, but I resented the demands it made upon me.

We stuck the paper onto a piece of half inch ply wood on the kitchen floor, it took a whole evening. We used P.V.A. glue, applying thin watery coats to each surface, letting each dry a little and then sticking the paper to the wood.

After that Sally and I began the finished artwork. She painted the map we had prepared, and with the help of the information in memo books I began drawing the border. Using references to flora, fauna and buildings, in those books, it became apparent what should be featured.

As with the paper, Lexie again did the telephoning round and found us the inks we needed, Pelican inks, a good range of colours and (most important) 'fade-fast'. We were all set to go now.

Sally and I worked whenever we were free, seldom at the same time, but often late into the night. Drawings and yet more drawings, transferring drawings onto the artwork, painting. It took a long time.

Next we needed a calligrapher. Lexie approached one 'professional' living locally who quoted an astronomic sum and whom we flatly refused. This was a project for love not money. A local schoolgirl, Claire Dell, just 17 years old, was known to have a fair hand. Lexie approached her and she said 'yes'. Poor Claire, what a brave girl she was to put pen to map, after all the colour work was completed.

Of course, before Claire could do anything we had to decide what went where. It wasn't easy, what do you put in, what do you leave out, of the information collected by the map group? More meetings.

Whilst all this artwork was going on, Lexie, our co-ordinator was endlessly making phone calls, contacts and arranging things. She managed to get us a grant from the Amenities and Countryside Committee of Devon County Council towards the cost of producing a poster of the map. This was quite a breakthrough from a local council and one which we were grateful for. The local village hall committee gave us a sum towards the cost of the frame. A sympathetic, local building firm took on the rest of the costs and making of the frame, from locally grown ash, Lexan, a perspex, replaced the glass.

Finally completion was in sight, about 9 months from that seed being planted. What a relief - it was finally on the village hall wall and out of my spare room. I must admit there was a gap in the household, the fourth child had grown up and left home.

Of course, the poster of the map had become another major facet of the project. One that has taken organisation by Lexie and energy from other members of the map group in terms of distribution and sales. It has certainly been a success, and to date we have handed several thousand pounds to projects in the Parish. And still the map sells.

Christine Case is a teacher and an artist.

The River Wear Map project: Sunderland Museum

Helen Sinclair

This large-scale textile map was made in 24 sections by different schools and shows the River Wear from Fatfield to the sea at Sunderland, a distance of 8 miles. The map itself is about 28 feet long by 7 feet high.

About 30 schools were involved in the project though only 21 completed sections of map. The youngest children to take part were 4 year olds from a reception class in an infants school, while the oldest were 15 year olds preparing for GCSE. In most cases the interest in the project spread far beyond the class who were officially involved and, in a couple of schools, almost every child took part. Two of Sunderland's special schools and an assessment unit were also involved. One of the many benefits of this successful project was the way in which special schools, infants, primary and secondary schools all contributed on equal terms. For the pupils from the special schools particularly there were important gains in confidence and self-esteem as a result.

The whole project took 8 months from initial planning to completion, and began in January with one day of in-service training for the teachers who had already committed themselves to the idea. They looked at ways of researching the map, learned different techniques of making it and planned their work programmes. Two crafts people - Margaret Williams, a knitter/textile designer with experience of orchestrating the Thirsk Parish Map, and Gillian Banks, a quilter - also worked with the teachers, passing on ideas and skills.

After this session each teacher was provided with a large-scale map of their particular stretch of river, plus a piece of hessian which was marked up with the margins and the shape of the river flowing through that particular section (a certain amount of geographical licence was needed to make the river flow due east-west while retaining its recognisable features!)

A second half-day Inset session at the end of the Spring term gave teachers the opportunity to expand on one particular skill or to research their own section more thoroughly. Most teachers finalised their plans over the Easter holiday and began work with the children and trips out to the riverside during the Summer term. The completed sections were brought into the Museum at the end of the Summer term, and after a week of frantic hemming and sewing, the whole map went on display in Sunderland Museum in August 1989.

It had been stressed to the teachers that the idea was not to produce an accurate geographical representation but to concentrate on features, buildings or patterns in the landscape that the children felt were important. One school's contribution included a fabric picture of a very cross teacher standing next to her broken-down car, immortalising an accident that happened on one of their trips out!

Another school incorporated a photograph of their class group, while others included history, legends or wild life. In the primary schools particularly the range of cross-curricular work was enormous including English, History, Science, Environmental Studies and Geography as well as Art & Design.

The techniques used to make the map were equally diverse. The only stipulation made was that the river itself should be done in finger knitting so that it was consistent throughout the whole length of the map. Otherwise teachers and children made their own decisions which included knitting, embroidery, quilting, rag rug making, weaving, wool-wrapping, fabric-painting, collage and other methods. As well as fabric and yarns they used plastic bags, card, wire, wood, string, toy cars and found objects.

The strength of a collaborative venture like this is that it is far more than the sum of its component parts. Everyone gained from working as a team and contributed to the overall result, but no one person can claim the credit for the successful outcome. Teachers were aware that if they backed out at a late stage and did not complete their section they were letting everyone down, yet at the same time they did not carry the overall responsibility for making the map a success. Everyone stretched themselves and did things and learned things as a group that they might not have attempted as individuals. For the children particularly there was the feeling that this was not something ephemeral, but something that would have a permanent place in the Museum and bring pleasure and benefit to the whole community. None of these things are measured in attainment targets, after the map was completed it still gives me (as Education Officer, who conceived the whole scheme) enormous pride and pleasure; the children who made it still regularly bring their parents and other relatives to check up on its progress, and the 150,000 annual visitors to the Museum who have taken the map to their hearts complain vigorously if the map has to be taken off display for a few months.

Overall the River Wear Map is a remarkable achievement and has received much praise and publicity. It has also generated enormous interest in schools outside Sunderland who have embarked on similar (though wisely less ambitious) projects. Schools in Gateshead, South Tyneside, Newcastle and North Tyneside have all used the River Wear Map as a stimulus for projects of their own.

The final vindication of a collaborative scheme like this is its cost. The total cost of the project, which involved more than 20 schools and lasted 8 months, was about £300. Approximately £200 of this was spent in fees to the two craftspeople involved; about £100 was spent on materials. The schools themselves paid for supply cover for the one and a half days Inset, though in many cases schools did not provide supplies and the teachers made their own arrangements on the basis "You cover for me today and I'll look after your class next time you go on an Inset course... The idea was put forward by the Education Officer at Sunderland Museum and supported by the Art Adviser and Humanities support teacher. The schools responded enthusiastically and the moral seems to be that a good arts project depends on ideas and imagination.

Anyone who has seen the River Wear Map is immediately struck by its vigour and energy and sheer *joie de vivre.* There is no doubt that its creation was a labour of love for the hundreds of schoolchildren who were involved with it, they still visit and show friends and parents, it remains a source of pleasure for the whole community.

Helen Sinclair is Principal Education Officer, Tyne & Wear Museums, Sunderland

Parish Maps in Shropshire

Hilary Hymas

In Shropshire the Community Council has been encouraging communities to undertake a Parish Maps Project and the Rural Arts Fieldworker has been working with local groups to help them get started.

In April 1990 a Parish Maps Day was held at Hadnall Village Hall when 120 people from all over Shropshire attended. The keynote speaker was Sue Clifford from Common Ground. Other contributors included Kate Evans from the Alvanley Parish Maps Project in Cheshire and countryside officers from the county planning and leisure departments. Examples of maps were on display and publications were on sale. It was a stimulating and lively occasion and ideas for several local maps were conceived.

At the Parish Maps Day, the Shropshire Parish Map Awards were launched, offering £1,000 in cash prizes to encourage local map projects. £500 in sponsorship was received from Shell UK, the remainder from West Midlands Arts and the Rural Development Commission, who have funded the post of Rural Arts Fieldworker at the Community Council. The final closing date for applications for the awards was 25 March 1991.

Funds were also available for Parish Map projects from the Rural Initiatives Fund, administered by the Community Council. Shropshire Leisure Services contributed £500 to this Fund for creative community maps, which provided much valued start-up grants.

Two all-day Parish Map workshops were organised to explore in more detail ways of tackling a map project and examining particular skills that could be used. The first one, at Harley Village Hall in July 1990, looked at using tape recorders and textiles in particular, with a wide range of possibilities to sample. Three visiting speakers led sessions for 20 participants from eight villages.

In December, a second workshop was held at Loppington Village Hall. This covered the use of photography in the morning session and in the afternoon two speakers, including the poet Eleanor Cooke, showed how to interpret landscape and our associations with it, in words and pictures, with examples from a map project in Cheshire. Twenty two people from ten different communities attended. Over a number of months in 1990 and 1991 the Rural Arts Fieldworker was invited to lead Parish Map sessions at village halls throughout Shropshire including Leebotwood, Rhydycroesau, Waters Upton, Little Stretton, Quatford, Chapel Lawn, Baschurch, Clive, Burford and Picklescott. Displays and talks were also given to Welshampton and Montford parish meetings and at Moreville, Sambrook and Alveley. Parish Map displays were mounted at Sellatyn, St Martins, Oswestry and Shrewsbury.

The judging of the Parish Map Awards took place in April 1991. A presentation evening and exhibition was held at the Shirehall, Shrewsbury in May when nine Awards were presented. A 45 minute live broadcast on Radio Shropshire prior to the presentations provided an opportunity for representatives of many of the projects to talk about their aims and what they had achieved. Ann Williams from Waters Upton was also interviewed on Radio 5.

A further exhibition of the Shropshire Parish Maps was held at the Gateway Arts Centre in Shrewsbury at the end of August 1991 for two and a half weeks.

A Brief Evaluation of the Project

The value of making a Parish Map is widely recognised and documented. The concept is open to a variety of interpretations and each project develops very individually, at its own pace and to its own criteria. The high profile given to Parish Maps by the Rural Arts Fieldworker and in particular the Parish Map Awards, provided a framework and timescale, within which new projects could flourish. The Award scheme added a strong incentive to some projects and helped to preserve a momentum and a target to aim for when work in progress might have tailed off.

The continuity of support and encouragement provided by the Rural Arts Fieldworker for communities embarking on a new venture was essential. Advice on how to get started, providing a factsheet on where to get further information and assistance, offering ideas and practical help and listening sympathetically when difficulties arose - all aspects of the kind of support provided. The workshops were much appreciated by those who attended and were a useful opportunity to exchange ideas. The financial support which the Rural Initiative Fund offered was vital in the early days of many projects. Even the quite small sums involved, in several cases, meant the viability of work going ahead.

The support and encouragement of local networks was also very important. Village Hall committees and Parish Councils all played their part. Projects were encouraged to gain the approval of the Parish Councils who in some cases were able to give small grants. Local fund-raising was important and had the added benefit of bringing the project to a wider audience and involving more people. There were instances where local firms provided goods at nominal cost.

The process of coming together on a community project has been of tremendous benefit to all the projects involved. In all cases a much greater awareness of their locality was mentioned. This in turn has led directly to other benefits for example a greater interest in the countryside, particularly footpaths, and an increased use and caring for the village hall. Map projects also developed as a way of integrating locals and newcomers.

It must be emphasised that although the finished map is of great value and can provide a focus for the community, the actual process of making a map, the local involvement, research and commitment that this entails is equally important. The discoveries we make about our locality, the local community and our role in it are of great benefit and perhaps, most important of all, that we can do things we never thought we could do.

The Parish Maps Project provided a useful focus for a number of different, smaller projects which developed, notably in Waters Upton, Baschurch, Rhydycroesau and Chapel Lawn. This allowed people with different interests and talents to concentrate on their particular area and allowed the whole project to be much more comprehensive. It also allows the projects to continue to develop.

In Waters Upton, for example, although the textile map is complete, the project continues with the development of a programme of parish walks and the preparation of a book to be published describing the walks and things of interest, the building up of a slide library and devising slide talks. In addition work is underway on a reminiscence project, interviewing local residents, some of which will be used to make a programme for Radio Shropshire. Other projects include a photographic record and surveys of flora and fauna. Not to mention social events in the village hall.

In Chapel Lawn, where the future of the village hall was threatened, the Parish Maps project has provided a much needed focus for a remote, scattered community. Although the idea of the map project aroused some opposition from locals at the outset, who saw it as a potential threat to their relatively isolated community by encouraging visitors, happily these fears have been overcome. They have been successful in involving children in the production of their map by organising workshops in the village hall.

A village party organised to increase involvement included a ceilidh, story-telling and a celebration of Candlemass. It was notable in being the first village celebration of its kind in 37 years. Chapel Lawn's ambitious plans to stage a musical (the map is to provide the back drop), 'The Ballad of Chapel Lawn' will draw on local material researched as part of the map project. Since the project started the use of the village hall has increased and there are plans to put any money raised by the musical back into the hall. "...the map has created a new focus in the village." *Liz Alker, Chapel Lawn*

The Parish Maps project in Baschurch has similarly developed in a number of different ways and has had a nucleus of very keen workers. They have had a harder task in involving the wider community in a large village with modern housing estates and more distractions. Their map will be placed in the village hall when it is completed, where it is sure to create some new interest. The photographic survey undertaken here, as in other villages, has been largely done by people whose previous experience of photography was limited to holiday snaps. They have now developed a keen eye for detail, seeing their surroundings with new understanding and appreciation.

Common Ground's aims, to encourage us to recognise and value the distinctiveness of our locality, even the everyday and the ordinary, and to conserve them, have been fostered in these projects. It is the first time many people have been involved in a project of this kind, which integrates the arts, environment and local history. Although a high degree of commitment is required to see a project through to completion, for those who can maintain an active interest, the benefits to themselves as well as the local community are considerable.

The Community Council will continue to encourage Parish Maps projects. We congratulate the achievements of the communities whose projects are mentioned here and also those which are in progress but not yet complete.

Waters Upton Parish Maps Project

The idea for a Parish Map came when two members of the Village Hall Committee attended an information day held in Hadnall Village Hall by the Community Council in April 1990. They were particularly impressed by the textile maps on show, the photographs of various villages and the footpath map and brochure produced by Hanwood. Having received a favourable response from several people locally, they went ahead and arranged a meeting in the Village Hall with Hilary Hymas providing display material, videos and a short talk. Sufficient people expressed an interest to get the project off the ground and the first real meeting took place at the end of June 1990.

It soon became clear that there were some very divergent ideas on what sort of map there should be and, since the project was aimed at bringing people together rather than causing discord, it was decided that each group should pursue its own particular interest. Material from the groups would be exchanged with other members and items published in the Parish Newsletter.

A change of Headteacher at the local school, which had just won a campaign against closure, brought the top class into the project with their own research history of the school. The chairman was asked to go along and talk to the children about Parish Maps in general and their project in particular. Just before Christmas she was invited back to a public performance of sketches based on the children's research into the log-book and records of the school at the turn of the century. There were written pieces, paintings, graphs, charts and computer analysis on display in addition to the sketches.

Meanwhile, those group members who were interested in making a textile map decided to press ahead with it. Only 4 members have been involved in the actual sewing - mainly for logistical reasons. Other members have helped by providing map enlargements, footpaths details, wild life details, photographs as a basis for paintings, background information and support in terms of money, materials and enthusiasm.

The map itself is intended as an index of all the other projects in which members are, or intend to be, involved. It contains the basic outline of roads, footpaths and rivers, the parish boundary - few people are aware of this since the parish was only created three years ago through Wrekin District Council - some notable buildings, road names and land-marks. It is designed so that additional subjects could be included later.

The surround is split into 4 areas depicting the different wild life habitats found - marsh, river, field, wood; agricultural activities in the area are shown in the top left-hand corner and the remainder contains plants, birds and buildings which could not be fitted in elsewhere. A variety of styles and methods have been used deliberately. It was particularly desired that the finished map should be colourful and attractive enough to hang in the Village Hall but that it should not become a 'precious' piece of craft which needed protection where the standard of work was so high that people would be discouraged from joining in the making of it.

Initial funds for the project came from the profits of the first year of the Parish Newsletter by way of a grant of £20. The Parish Council gave a grant of £30 and the Rural Initiatives Fund £50 (£100 grant aid in total). A Cheese and Wine Evening raised a further £75.89 as well as providing an opportunity for groups to display their work so far. Meetings are held of the whole group - whoever can make it - on the first Monday evening of the month (except Bank Holidays). Our main problem is trying to get very busy people together. Some members have outside commitments which take precedence over meetings, others find work or family commitments arise at short notice. Usually, we have 8 - 10 members present and others provide news, material or comments to be passed on even if they cannot attend. We particularly try to maintain an easy-going atmosphere - we want to enjoy doing this

- and some people have never attended a full meeting. The interest groups are left very much to sort out their own timetables and methods. The fact of having to tell the whole group that no progress has been made proves quite an effective stimulus. Members help each other in many ways providing equipment or materials (one member used an overhead projector to enlarge the outline of the textile map to the required size) - even going to the County Records Office for one member who is disabled and finds the access very difficult - providing transport, passing on messages, minutes, etc, typing, photocopying or marking material for other members. Personally, I feel that the greatest contribution is often the support and encouragement provided for other people's efforts.

The textile map is largely complete and will be hanging in the Hall for the open evening on April 12th. It is, however, only the end of the beginning. The wild life project has an initial time-scale of one year's observation, the audio map is promised to Radio Shropshire for early 1992. The photo-record is well-advanced but the accompanying house to house questionnaire has only just begun. The first footpath walk takes place on 24th March and it is hoped to cover every route during the summer so that the brochure can be produced during next winter. Input to this comes from both the wild life and the historical groups as well as material gathered by the audio and photo-record groups. The school has continued to be involved as much as the new National Curriculum will allow and hopes to do its own wild life project in the Summer Term. The next open meeting may well produce new members with new ideas - if so they will be welcomed. We are a small, scattered community who have already discovered that we have much more in common than we thought we had.

Ann Williams, Waters Upton, 1991

The Waters Upton project received first prize in the Parish Map Awards. They used their prize money to publish a brochure on local walks of interest and to produce a postcard of their map.

Hilary Hymas is the Rural Arts Field worker for the Community Council of Shropshire

Putting Devon on the Map

Bob Butler

For some reason I have always loved maps. Ever since childhood, while my friends were busy devouring 'Swallows and Amazons', I was to be found under the bedclothes with my favourite atlas or a fanciful map of the early African explorers. The attraction has to do with a fascination for what Lawrence Durrell, and many since, have termed the 'sense of place'. So many places, every one unique, and all demanding attention - I found it irresistible then and I still do. The thrill of discovering a new place with its own history and set of particular circumstances; its own smell, accent, points of arrival....its very own place in the world. Good maps can convey so much and can whet the appetite for being there and, truly, maps and places are inseparable for when a place disappears 'off the map' it may be gone forever.

I came across my first Parish Map some years ago when working in Dorset and I became an immediate devotee. It seemed to me that here was a medium that offered so many possibilities both in terms of enriching local knowledge and a sense of belonging and in terms of creative expression. A couple of years later I joined the Beaford Centre, a community arts organisation in blissful North Devon, and, with the invaluable help and support of Common Ground, I quickly took the opportunity to establish what I believe was the first Local Distinctiveness residency in the country. As this programme was devoted to exploring concepts of place and local people's responses to their own community it was inevitable that we would encounter Parish Maps along the way. What surprised me, though, was quite how many maps there were, either complete or in progress, and how easy it was to encourage other groups and communities to embrace the idea. I quickly discovered that what amounted to a mass movement was taking place throughout Devon. Apart from our own humble efforts in the north of the county many communities had been inspired by Common Ground's campaign, including groups such as the Devon Federation of Women's Institutes and the Environment Service of South Hams District Council.

I felt it was time to bring all this energy and enthusiasm together and so I began planning an exhibition of Parish Maps from throughout Devon. Using a number of established contacts I managed to collate a data base of over 120 map projects. Most were complete, some works in progress, others merely embryonic. I wrote to each of the 'mappers', enclosing a simple questionnaire, asking whether they would consider exhibiting their map in an exhibition at our Plough Arts Centre in Great Torrington. Almost all said that they would be delighted, in fact several came to visit me personally, travelling many miles across the county, to explain about 'their' map and its history. The groups, almost without exception, took enormous pride in their achievement and, by inference, in the community which their map represented.

In the end we were able to take 70 or so maps for display and these were exhibited for almost three weeks in the arts centre, attracting a great deal of local and regional interest. On the opening day we arranged a number of talks and practical demonstrations of the craft of mapping as well as an out-and-about session when about 30 people braved the pouring rain for a tour of Torrington, during which they were given advice on how to translate the physical environment into map form. As well as most of the mappers themselves, over 400 people visited the Plough that day.

What was staggering about the exhibition, apart from the superb quality of the maps themselves, was the variety of techniques and styles which had been employed in their execution. Many were straight-forward paintings, mostly watercolour or acrylic, but invariably highly detailed. Some were representational, focusing on themes or events rather that geographical accuracy. There were many textile and fabric maps, photographic collages, pen and ink drawings, three-dimensional papier maché models, even a ceramic map made up of a series of interlocking ceramic tiles. They had been produced by schools, Womens' Institutes, parish councils, village hall committees, local history societies and all manner of other community groups, often established specifically for the purpose. It has to be admitted that most would not have made the Royal Academy but given that few were actually produced by professional artists the overall standard, artistically, was high. A handful were exceptional and almost certainly represent the highest form of contemporary artistic expression witnessed in their respective communities. This is some achievement and helps to explain the degree of pride which these otherwise refreshingly unpretentious groups took in the product of their endeavour.

The maps themselves though only tell part of the story. Many of the groups had been beavering away for months, some for years. They had worked hard to involve as many people with local knowledge as possible and had tried to encourage all sections and interest groups in the community to contribute something. Many of the tapestries had been designed specifically with this in mind, with groups or individuals each taking responsibility for a small panel or square of fabric. One group even raised money for their project by 'selling stitches' at the village fete. These kinds of initiative are important because ultimately Parish Maps, like the communities themselves, need to be owned by the many not by the few. If we are to look after what is special to us, what we really care for, this will only happen if those of us who are not born with the privilege of absolute power speak with a collective voice. Most of the Devon Parish Maps are displayed prominently 'back home' in village halls or community centres. Only one, that I know of, is not in the public domain and this is due entirely to artistic pique.

Many map projects have expanded to encompass other community activities. Several groups have written booklets describing their village or parish, mostly concerned with local history but some went into great detail about wild life, buildings and landscape features. Others actually chronicled the work that went into producing the map itself. Many of the maps have also been transformed into prints, postcards, greeting cards, tea towels and place mats. One ingenious group have even explored the possibility of scanning their map onto a computer and then liberating it on the Internet.

So that was our exhibition and despite the hard work which was involved I can genuinely say that it was a truly invigorating experience and one which could and should be repeated in other parts of the country. And why stop there? When I mentioned the idea of a Parish Map to some friends in Arizona recently they decided that something similar was just what their community needed. I must call to find out how far they've got!

Bob Butler is the Director of the Beaford Arts Centre, Beaford, North Devon.

"....What do you consider the ***largest*** *map that would be really useful?"*
"About six inches to the mile."
"Only ***six inches:****" exclaimed Mein Herr. "We very soon got to six* ***yards*** *to the mile. Then we tried a* ***hundred*** *yards to the mile. And then came the grandest idea of all! We actually made a map of the country, on the scale of* ***a mile to the mile****!"*

"Have you used it much?" I enquired.
"It has never been spread out, yet," said Mein Herr; "the farmers objected: they said it would cover the whole country, and shut out the sunlight! So we now use the country itself, as its own map, and I assure you it does nearly as well."

Sylvie and Bruno Concluded (The Man in the Moon) Lewis Carroll

Some Common Ground Publications

from place to PLACE: maps and Parish Maps, Sue Clifford and Angela King, eds. 1996, £10 + £1.25 p&p

Parish Maps, 24 page pamphlet, A5 full colour, 1996, £2.50 inc p&p

Parish Maps, A4 folded leaflet, free with s.a.e. (£1 for 10)

Parish Maps Slide Pack, 20 slides + commentaries and pamphlet, £30

Local Distinctiveness: Place, Particularity and Identity, Sue Clifford and Angela King, eds. 1993, £5.95 + £1.25 p&p

Places: the city and the invisible, Sue Clifford, PADT, 1993, £10.99 inc p&p

Celebrating Local Distinctiveness by Common Ground for Rural Action, £2.20 inc p&p

Common Ground Rules for Local Distinctiveness - an ABC of the locally particular, (illustrated broadsheet, colour, A2) £4.50 inc p&p

New Milestones: Sculpture, Community and the Land, Joanna Morland, 1988, £4.95 + £1.05 p&p

In A Nutshell: a manifesto for trees and a guide to growing and protecting them, Neil Sinden, 1989, £6.95 + £1.40 p&p

Orchards a guide to local conservation, 1989, £4.95 + £1.05 p&p

The Apple Source Book, particular recipes for diverse apples, 1991, £4.95 + 75p p&p

Apple Games and Customs, Beatrice Mayfield, 1994, £6.95 inc. p&p

The Apple Broadcast, 16 page newspaper all about the Save our Orchards and Apple Day projects, 1994 £2.00 inc p&p

Apple Map full of wonderful illustrations and descriptions of many varieties of apples county by county, A1 colour, £7.00 inc p&p

The Art of Gentle Gardening - thoughts on Linking Plants, People and Places, 24 page pamphlet, full colour, 1995, £2.00 inc p&p

Local Flora Britannica pamphlet, 32 pages full colour, 1995, £2.50 inc p&p

An Introduction to the Deeds & Thoughts of Common Ground, £2.50 + 50p p&p

Common Ground leaflet - free with s.a.e. (£1 for 10)

Exhibitions illustrating some of Common Ground's projects including Parish Maps, New Milestones and Orchards, are available for hire. Please send s.a.e. for further details.

Common Ground, Seven Dials Warehouse,
44 Earlham Street, London WC2H 9LA

Parish Maps

Common Ground

Parish Maps help express what you value as a community, and are a first step to standing up for your place.

Muchelney Parish Map © Gordon Young 1987

Muchelney, Somerset

The question "What do you value in your place?" turns everyone into experts. From the smallest of details to the most enduring stories, no one else can dictate what is important to you, - the lovely doors along the row, Geoff's Hedge and how he keeps the holly trimmed, the pollarded willows, the sluice gates, orchards and wandering chickens; seasonal things - such as where the best blackberries or mushrooms can be found, Jim ploughing that way, where the toads spawn, the floods; events that have become stories - "do you remember when lightning struck the holm oak?". All of these and many more are captured by Gordon Young's Parish Map of Muchelney. It could not be anywhere else. (pen & wash 2'x3')

Parish Maps

Places and Values

Everywhere means something to someone. You don't have to own it, or even see it everyday, for a place, and its stories to be important to you. The combination of commonplace histories and ordinary nature makes places what they are. Things do not have to be spectacular, rare or endangered for people to value them and want them about their everyday lives.

Whether you live in a town, a city or in the country, there are some things around you which are part of your daily round. Perhaps there are buildings which seem 'at home' in the landscape because they reflect the lives of the people who lived in the area before you - a mill, a line of houses, a quay or railway station. Perhaps you enjoy a walk along lanes lined with primroses in spring, through water meadows or wild fells grazed by sheep; your walk may take you between the ducks on the canal and red brick warehouses, or through the sounds and smells of the street market to school. Wherever you are, it is the details and overlays which have meaning to you and which give your area its own local distinctiveness.

Making a Parish Map can help people to come together to chart the things that they value locally, to make their voice heard amongst professionals and developers, to inform and assert their need for nature and culture on their own terms, and to begin to take action and some control in shaping the future of their place.

Coming together to make a Parish Map can help to inform, to embolden and to change things. We need a better democracy - more local, more pliable, more responsive - and it is we who have to forge it, to take responsibility into action.

What is a Parish Map?

A Parish Map demonstrates what people claim as their own locality and what they value in it - wild life, history, work, landmarks, buildings, people, festivals. It does not have to be precise or cartographically correct, but by illustrating locally distinctive activities and features, it helps you to focus on the everyday things that make your place significant to you and different from the next. It can include the elusive responses which cannot be measured or counted and also the invisible - the stories, dialect, names and fragments of everyone's history.

Parish Maps are a starting point for local action, they are demonstrative, subjective statements made by and for a community, exploring and showing what it cares

Detail of Elham Parish Map © The Elham Circle, 1994

Elham, Kent

Members of the Elham Circle decided thay wanted to produce a footpath map, but soon became carried away with how much they wanted to include, so decided a Parish Map was far more appropriate. The map is a painting, 8 feet long. None of those involved were artists, but felt they wanted to create the map as well as collect all the information. With a grant from Rural Action they were able to approach Graham Clarke, a local artist, who gave them tuition and other practical help.

"We in the Elham Circle felt that the production of the map was very worthwhile, it brought us closer together and made us more aware of our beautiful valley. We are currently updating all 56 of our footpaths and doing conservation work in the chalk pit area, so its all had a knock on effect."

They are now making map to celebrate the chalk flora they have discovered, which will be published at the annual flower festival. (8'x4' triptych, painting on board) about in its locality. They offer a way of communicating creatively and socially how rich everyday places are, and what importance seemingly ordinary things have to everyone. All kinds of people old and young, from varied cultural backgrounds, by sharing their ideas and knowledge, begin to cherish their locality more and often become involved directly in its care. Parish Maps can be made by anyone, in any way, of any place.

Why Parish?

'Parish' is offered not to define but to describe the scale at which people feel a sense of familiarity and ownership in their place. We have no word in English to express bro or cynefin in Welsh or heimat in German. Common Ground suggests the word 'Parish' in the same vein: home place, your own familiar territory, the neighbourhood to which you feel a sense of belonging, the locality which 'belongs' to you. You may wish to draw your own line around your street or estate, you may be challenged by the old ecclesiatical, newer civil parish or community council boundaries or you may allow your map to fray at the edges - it is up to you to describe your 'Parish'.

Initiating a Parish Map

Anyone can initiate a Parish Map. Individuals or established civic society, environment, local history, social or arts organizations have acted as the catalyst, or a specially formed Parish Map group might promote it. It will help you and your community to discover more about, and make known to others, what is important to you. Displaying the map in a public place will provoke continuing discussion.

In some areas the parish, district, borough or community councils have offered support, excited by the opportunity to foster a sense of local identity and to encourage local people to have a say in planning the future for their place. County, Borough and District Councils in Hertfordshire, Cleveland, Taunton Deane and South Hams have promoted their own projects, and toured displays hired from Common Ground to libraries, village halls and schools. Others have organised exhibitions or workshops, as part of their public participation exercises and increasingly in their Local Agenda 21 and Parish Paths initiatives. The same has been done by many of the Community Councils such as Warwickshire, Buckinghamshire, Somerset and Shropshire and groups as well as community arts and wild life trusts. The Countryside Council for Wales used the Parish Maps idea in their y Jigsô Lleol (the Local Jigsaw).

On a more informal level the project has spread by word of mouth. The makers of the Uplyme Parish Map have been invited by groups and Parish Councils across

Devon, Somerset and Dorset to pass on their experience. In Hertfordshire many have been inspired by Croxley Green's Parish Map and the co-ordinator Margaret Pomfret has given talks and encouragement. Womens Institute's have become involved in the same way, seeing exhibitions elsewhere and taking the idea back to their own Federations.

A Parish Map can be made by an individual, but the making and the map itself will be richer if they provoke discussion and reflect many points of view. Some mappers have created groups to walk, talk and gather information and views on different topics and then all come together to make the map. Sometimes a local artist or cartographer has been commissioned to use all of this material to turn into the map or been paid to help with design, offer tuition and keep the momentum going. Any co-ordinating group should try to draw in as many people as they can. While the map may be completed the mapping never ends - values change, new people move in and places are developing all the time.

Tow Law , County Durham

This map was designed and painted by people of this small town, with help from local artist, Romney Chaffer, and funding from W.E.A, Tow Law Town Council and Wear Valley District Council. A great deal of information was gathered from the local history society, schools and local people. It is easy to read, showing the town, agriculture and industry past, present and future and hangs in the busy Community Centre. The project has been continued in wall hangings and murals which celebrate the town. (7'x9' acrylic on canvas)

Through making a Parish Map you can identify what your place has to offer and exchange ideas on what needs more attention. For example: do you have access to good local networks of foot or cycle paths? Your place might be dominated by flood meadows, heathland, deciduous woodland, abandoned mine workings, unused corners in the city, wild areas in the park: is there an abundance of wild life and particular habitats? Could the hedgerows or verges be richer? In the city or country, can you play or sit by the river or a clear stream? Are the old buildings in good repair, are there any grants to help? Is ordinary history recognised and protected? Could a Parish Map help to attract sympathetic tourism? Where should new development be allowed? What about the potential for community use - a field, orchard, allotments, old chapel? Could the owner be offered help - in exchange for some access? Do you know where the Parish Boundary goes? If it follows banks and hedges, or a curving city street with big trees these features could be very old and have historical and wild life value accumulated over many centuries doubling their importance to the locality. When did people last Beat the

Easton, Bristol

The community arts group Vizability Arts worked with Easton's multi ethnic community, to create a Parish Map over a two week period. The map was taken round on a double decker bus to encourage all residents to participate. Being on the bus gave a great sense of occasion, making it an event in itself and there was much talking, singing and swapping of stories from the older residents. The map now has a permanent home at the Easton Community Centre. (Batik, 8'x8')

Bounds? Are there existing festivals or could you create new celebrations for your locality? What makes your place different from the next? How can you express its particular identity and encourage builders, farmers and local authorities to reinforce local distinctiveness?

Getting started

Are you interested in natural history, geography, food, customs, stories, local history, industrial archaeology, landscape, literature, buildings, walking, ethnic landmarks, people's history? You might start with any of these or you may begin with no categories in mind but agree to photograph parts of your place, each to sleuth different sub-territories or to come together over a cup of tea and a big sheet of paper and start talking, noting and marking the things you know and which are significant to you.

You may want to use an Ordnance Survey map of your area to act as a guide - the 1:2,500 maps offer a good start. It may be helpful to look at old maps in the county or borough record office, the archivists are most helpful and the treasures they unearth are full of interest.

Any skill can prove useful to make a Parish Map. They should be expressive, any size and shape, don't feel constrained by conventional mapping scales, sizes and methods. Parish Maps have been sewn, woven, knitted, printed, drawn, painted, filmed, animated, sung, acted and written. The point is that it helps you to communicate with each other and demonstrates your view of your place.

Think of ways of getting people involved and at least let everyone know that you or your group is planning to make a Parish Map. Make contact with local organisations - WI, photography clubs, tenants groups, schools, allotment or civic societies, evening classes and retirement groups.

People come to events rather than meetings. Link a local event with a display of Parish Maps and offer food and drink. The people of Chideock held coffee mornings where people could swap stories, old photos and memories. Ask people to bring ideas and information for the next gathering and make these a regular event in the local calendar.

Invite people to discuss ideas in the pub, village hall, community centre or on walks. Don't reject anything, at least not at the early gatherings. Ask Parish Mappers from other places to come and talk to your group.

Find out what people would like to include on the map. Offer a simple challenge to all inhabitants via the local shop, pub, school or library. In Redlynch, 900 questionnaires were sent out with the milkman, to be returned at the sub-post office. Go to meetings of other local groups ask for their ideas and collaboration.

Finding Time

There is no special time for deciding to make a Parish Map, however it may prove easier to raise interest for the project if it links to a celebration, this could be a new one, such as Apple Day or an old one, either currently practised or reinvented such as Beating the Bounds.This ancient ritual, a lesson in geography before maps were commonplace, has been forgotten in many places. Yet it is a perfect way of socially exploring the edges of your place, and passing on knowledge across generations (although you may not wish to perpetuate the 'rememberings' which involve beatings with sticks or throwings into nettle patches). Territorial disputes these days are fought elsewhere, but to take stock annually of the health of the local environment; to make note of the landmark trees, stones, streams, and other boundary markers; and to create a time for the passing on of knowledge down generations and from established families to newcomers, gives a modern importance to the idea.

In order to achieve a boundary walk, you need a map and preparation which takes you to all landowners whose land and water need to be crossed. In Cambridge the ancient Rogation Walk takes enthusiasts through the middle of Marks and Spencers. Many a boundary has no rights of way along it. This alone is an adventure and has much potential for building relationships and new access.

The Devon Federation of WI's used their 75th Anniversary celebrations as a way of promoting the project, about seventy maps were made and shown at Stover school in July 1995. Many Parish Councils finished or launched Parish Maps in 1994 as a way of marking their centenary. The projects have introduced these groups to a wider community or vice versa, and are leading to much more.

The most successful maps reflect the jumble of overlapping interests and the jostle of varied values - some offer criticisms, most have a strong feeling for geography, history and nature. Every locality has its own enthusiasts and personalities: feast makers, extroverts, writers, needleworkers, map users, artists, hoarders and collectors, historians, geologists, wild life activists, organisers, entertainers, calligraphers, computer buffs, walkers. Everyone's skills are important, everyone's values are needed.

The River Wear Map © courtesy of Tyne & Wear Museums 1989, (two sections out of four), West and East (facing page)

The River Wear Map, Sunderland, Tyne & Wear

Sunderland Museum Education Service ran an extremely successful Parish Map project in 1989, which involved twenty one schools, both primary and secondary. Each school was asked to map their patch along a nine mile stretch of the north and south banks of the River Wear which runs through the centre of the city. Many different fabric techniques were used, the only specification was that the river must be in finger knitting.

For the first time these schools had a sense of each other (apart from through sport) and an identification with the whole city. Although each school designed and made their own section, they had to talk to one another about the exact positioning of roads and

other details that crossed over. The project was highly ambitious, but as each piece was a manageable size, the scale of the complete map was not overwhelming. A trust was built up between the schools , no one could drop out or not finish their section or else the whole project would have failed. Schools were given a few months before they had to commit themselves, but once they had there was no turning back!

The map toured to each school then found a permanent home in the museum, where the children, now teenagers, some even with their own young families, still come into look at it and point out the pieces they did. The current schoolchildren often see that they value the same details as a generation before them. (30'x8', textile)

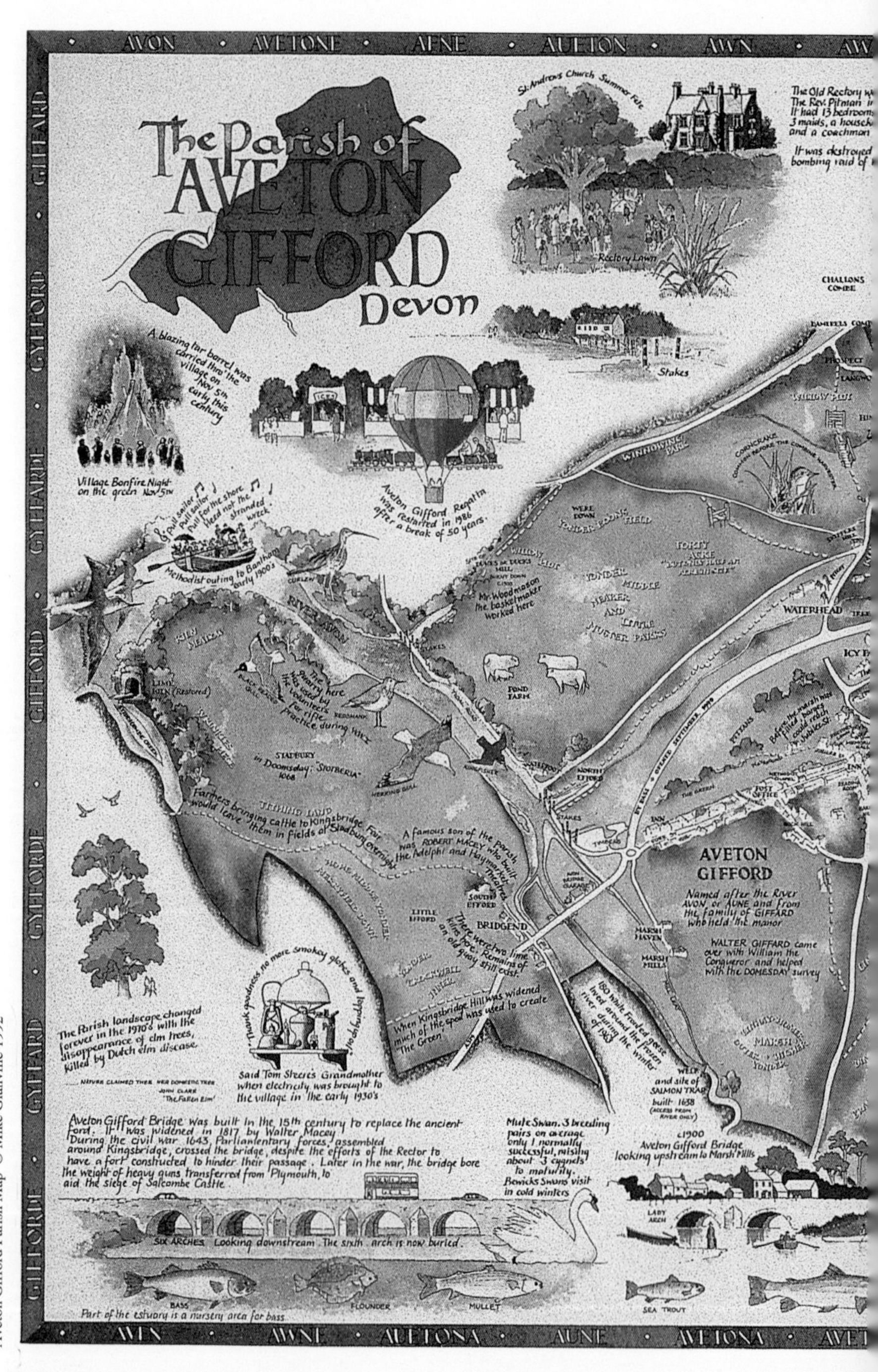

Aveton Gifford Parish Map © Mike Glanville 1992

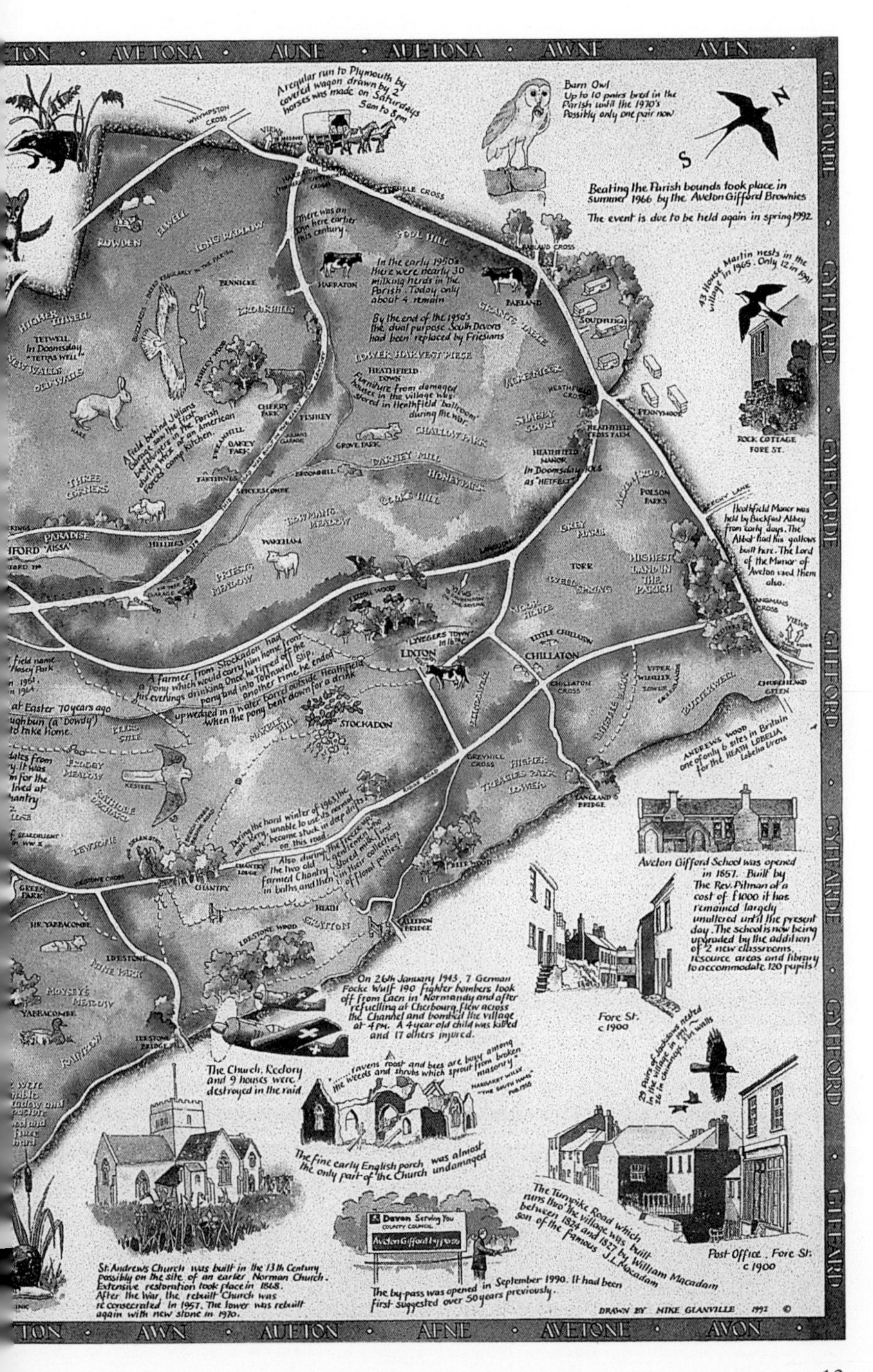
AVETONA · AUNE · AUETONA · AWNE · AVEN
GIFFORDE · GYFFARD · GYFFORDE · GIFFORD · GYFFARDE · GYFFORD · GIFFARD
AWN · AUETON · AFNE · AVETONE · AVON
A regular run to Plymouth by covered wagon drawn by 2 horses was made on Saturdays 5am to 8pm
Barn Owl
Up to 10 pairs bred in the Parish until the 1970's
Possibly only one pair now
N
S
Beating the Parish bounds took place in summer 1966 by the Aveton Gifford Brownies
The event is due to be held again in spring 1992.
43 House Martin nests in the village in 1965. Only 12 in 1991
ROCK COTTAGE FORE ST.
There was an iron here earlier this century
In the early 1950's there were nearly 30 milking herds in the Parish. Today only about 4 remain
By the end of the 1950's the dual purpose South Devons had been replaced by Friesians
Furniture from damaged houses in the village was stored in Heathfield 'ballroom' during the war
HEATHFIELD MANOR
In Doomsday 1086 as "HETFELT"
Heathfield Manor was held by Buckfast Abbey from early days. The Abbot had his gallows built here. The Lord of the Manor of Aveton used them also.
TETWELL
In Doomsday "TETAS WELL"
A field behind Julians Garage saw the first beefburgers in the Parish during WW2 at an American Forces camp kitchen.
HIGHEST LAND IN THE PARISH
A farmer from Stockadon had a pony which would carry him home from his evenings drinking. Once he tipped off the pony and into Townswell Slip, another time he ended up wedged in a water barrel outside Heathfield when the pony bent down for a drink
LIXTON
CHILLATON
STOCKADON
ANDREWS WOOD
one of only 6 sites in Britain for the HEATH LOBELIA
Lobelia Urens
During the hard winter of 1963 the milk lorry, unable to use its normal route, became stuck in deep drifts on this road
Also during the freeze-up the two old gentlemen who farmed Chantry stored milk first in baths and then in their collection of floral potties!
CHANTRY
Aveton Gifford School was opened in 1857. Built by The Rev. Pitman at a cost of £1000 it has remained largely unaltered until the present day. The school is now being upgraded by the addition of 2 new classrooms, resource areas and library to accommodate 120 pupils
Fore St. c1900
On 26th January 1943, 7 German Focke Wulf 190 fighter bombers took off from Caen in Normandy and after refuelling at Cherbourg flew across the Channel and bombed the village at 4pm. A 4 year old child was killed and 17 others injured.
The Church, Rectory and 9 houses were destroyed in the raid
"......ravens roost and bees are busy among the weeds and shrubs which sprout from broken masonry"
The fine early English porch was almost the only part of the Church undamaged
The Turnpike Road which runs thro' the village was built between 1824 and 1827 by William Macadam son of the famous J.L. Macadam
Post Office, Fore St. c1900
St. Andrews Church was built in the 13th Century possibly on the site of an earlier Norman Church. Extensive restoration took place in 1868. After the war, the rebuilt Church was re consecrated in 1957. The tower was rebuilt again with new stone in 1970.
Devon Serving You
COUNTY COUNCIL
Aveton Gifford by-pass
The by-pass was opened in September 1990. It had been first suggested over 50 years previously.
DRAWN BY MIKE GLANVILLE 1992 ©

Aveton Gifford, Devon *(previous page)*
Aveton Gifford villagers awoke on Thursday morning to the strange sound of silence - the bypass had been opened the day before and the high street was once more theirs. A great party with trestle tables and large amounts of food thoroughly reclaimed the street. Reinvigorated, the Parish Council approached their District Council to make a leaflet for them, to encourage people to explore the place on foot.

The South Hams Environment Service suggested instead that the residents make a Parish Map for themselves and that the council would help by printing it: "in the process it is hoped that local people will create far more than a map - but shall discover the place for themselves and highlight some of the features they would like to conserve or improve, turning community art into community action."

At a video show of the street party, a core group was formed who encouraged people to gather together their feelings on wild life, history, buildings, trees and more.

"What's special about Aveton Gifford?" asked artist Sally Tallant faced with a class of 8 to 10 year old pupils from the school. "Tell me what you like, what you don't like and why". With that she and two members of the Environment Service left the classroom each led by a small group of excited and intrigued youngsters.

The story continues: "As we were taken around, we learnt which trees were important. The 'face tree' had a face on its bark, and its low bending limbs were easily climbed. Pampas grass would hide you from invading tribes and, in the middle of the stream, elvers could be found clinging like ribbons around a pebble, yet disappearing at a touch. Led by our guides, we found hollow hedgerow trees where you could lose your arm right up to the shoulder, drain covers and paving slabs which made patterns of flowers and diamonds, and a collection of derelict barns which were haunted. Certainly ghostly giggles could be heard as soon as we got near! Quick-sighted and sharply observant, the children could teach many a long-standing resident to see the village with new eyes."

Elsewhere other research parties wandered the parish. Many evening jaunts ended up in the pub, the conversations echoed around the place. They ran a photographic workshop resulting in an exhibition with a slide show of rare archive photos - it prompted lots of memories.

Mike Glanville, a local artist took on the hard work of bringing together the map, which the South Hams District Council printed. They have revived Beating the Bounds. The local baker reinvented Rammalation biscuits, which were customary fare on Rogation Sunday, by making the 'Aveton Gifford Bun' and special ale - Ganging Beer was brewed.

The core group still meet regularly and have produced two illustrated walks leaflets and sales of these and prints of the map are helping to restore buildings of interest in the village for public use. The map which is acrylic on paper, has been printed as posters, which have sold well, both locally and abroad. (3'6"x2'6", acrylic on paper)

Thirsk, North Yorkshire *(overpage)*

"The idea started with Civic Society concern over the proposed development of a supermarket on the nearby nursery site. Things can all too easily disappear before people realise what is happening and are able to do anything about it, so we decided to illustrate what people value most in the community, and the map will now be a permanent record. It will have a powerful influence on future development where people might be unaware of the importance of what the community did not want destroyed or damaged. People would be able to tell developers: 'Here it is on the map.' I am sure that if outside developers had some idea before they make plans for an area just how the community feels, they would think twice before investing their money in destroying things that other people value. The map is a public statement, a celebration of where we live.

For about two years the upstairs room in the town library became a veritable hive of activity for much of the background work. People of all ages sitting round together sewing, knitting, embroidering and chatting about the locality.

It was a marvellous community effort and really quite amazing to see what people came up with. Not just public buildings or famous landmarks, but flowers and animals. For instance the kingfisher that sometimes appears by the river, features twice on the map. Even the famous White Horse at Kilburn, which we cannot actually see from here, appears, I suspect, for symbolic rather than factual reasons. Since its inception the map has become a major talking point. It has provoked much comment like: 'Where is Bribery Terrace, and how did it get its name?' and 'I have never seen sheep in Front Street.' It shows how much people can miss about their own town, until it is pointed out to them.

We felt the map was the best way of ensuring it all for posterity. After all, it illustrates our uniqueness." Joe Salmon, one of the co-ordinators of the Thirsk Parish Map and the main spokesperson.

Money was raised to fund Margaret Williams, a textile artist from Middlesborough, to help with design and making. The map demonstrates a huge range of different techniques, including knitting, ragging, embroidery and tapestry, all threads and materials were given by a local firm, added to, from many local ragbags. It measures 24' long and is made in four sections, each also depicting one of the four seasons. The villages of Kilvington, Carlton Minniott and Sowerby are included, as well as the market town of Thirsk, which together make up the Parish. The Cod Beck, a river running through all four gives a central theme and links the pieces together.

The map took around nine months to make and nearly everyone in the community became involved along the way. It now has a permanent place in the library and has even been taken to a public inquiry to try and prevent the erection of pylons around the town. On this occasion the map, which is heavy, the sections being joined with velcro, began to give with a huge ripping sound, as if it too was giving its voice against this unsympathetic development. The mappers knew exactly what this was, but the inspector was visibly moved and insisted they set it down carefully. The decision is still awaited. (24'x6', textile)

Thirsk Parish Map © Thirsk Civic Society, 1989. Left to right, top:Spring, Summer; bottom: Autumn, Winter

Keeping Going

Welcome any offer of information and help. If you can't fit all the information gathered on the map you may be able to use it in a parish chest or book or to create future projects. There will be crucial debates on what to put in and what to leave out. You may agree to disagree. You could use the same literature to create local walks leaflets, a Parish Alphabet, a local history or wild life guide, or print postcards with extracts from the map or you may find these are ways of beginning.

Encourage spin off groups. The point is to go beyond making the map, to become involved in caring for your locality in whatever way you wish.

Keep the momentum going with events and use them to provide you with supplies of help and information: a slide show of old photos to prompt memories, walking and talking led by established residents or children; walks and gatherings with an archaeologist, lichen expert, architect, social historian to exchange knowledge, explain odd corners and raise new areas of interest (Rural Action and some local authorities will give grants to help you bring local experts in on your own terms); children's games; displays of local collections; wild life surveys; cooking demonstrations of local recipes using local plants; have a stall or display at local events, the raft race, church fete, school open day, Christmas fair, garden festival, library or market.

Parish Maps and creative action

The Parish Map should be hung in a public place - the community centre, school, village hall, library, museum, church, local shop or pub - to act as a continuing stimulus to discussion, inspiring us to look again at our surroundings and to discover new ways of encouraging responsibility for ordinary but well loved places. Try to decide how and where the map will be displayed while mapping is in progress and gain clear commitments from the relevant body or committee.

Campaign for improvements in the locality, things highlighted by the map making - such as more directed lights so you can feel safer at night but do not lose your view of the stars, or single deck buses so that the trees can spread more, arresting development on the water meadows and restoring the sluices instead to encourage wild flowers and swallows. Perhaps you will want to start new traditions or reinvent old ones, such as Wassailing, Field Days or egg rolling.

Hundreds of maps have been made by environment, parish, women's, elderly, play, community, wild life, arts, craft, school and special groups. Parish Maps have become a social focus and an agenda for action.

Alveston Parish Council near Bristol began their map work by walking and then finding they had to clear their footpaths, having discovered, many routes were blocked or in poor repair. With the help of local farmers they found out who owned all the land and became familiar with their parish boundary. They reported to Avon County Council Highways Dept. the number of stiles, bridges, paths that needed repairing, clearing or installing. At first the council sent their own officers out to check the work was necessary, but soon came to trust the group's judgements. The farmers installed and made necessary repairs, 132 in all, undergrowth was cleared and all paths were officially declared open. The Parish Map was printed to help publicise the network and to prevent the paths falling back into disrepair. Northavon District Council helped fund this and are helping with up-keep of the paths, as are local ramblers groups. Two walks leaflets have been produced, communal walks organised and a Rogation Service held which will be repeated.

Oswestry Parish Mappers at work, 1996

Oswestry, Shropshire

An ambitious Parish Map in seven sections made as part of a rehabilitation programme at Lorne Street Day Centre. The map has been very positive. "When we're working together people don't look down on us, we're looking across at each other as equals."

Chideock Parish Map, © Chideock Society painted by Gillian M Moores 1990

Chideock, Dorset

"The village lies by the sea, and has become a busy holiday place, its numbers more than double in the summer and autumn. A period of retrieval happens over the few winter months, when the place preens its tattered traces, gathers its memories and re-asserts its own identity, before the next season of demands deluges and dilutes its personality again. Those who live there felt just about in control, but plans to extend yet further the caravan park and the season, filled people with fears of final drowning".

Inspired by the Uplyme Parish Map, the Chideock Society involved people with passions in history, nature and much more to create their own, over two years. It shows what they value, both for themselves and tourists who visit. A photographic record was made of all the streets in the parish as a starting point, followed by questions and teas held in the village hall. A good deal of positive action and activity has been initiated through the mapping to try and keep the growth in tourism at a controllable level, paid for in part by proceeds from the printed map. (watercolour 4'x4')

In Lockwood, (Cleveland) subsidence flashes with their wild life have been secured from council rubbish dumping; trees, hedgerows and ponds in Fryent Park, (London Borough of Brent) have been saved from destruction; public inquiries fought in Golden Hill (Bristol); in Redlynch, (Wiltshire) buildings renovated; in Chartham, (Kent) an orchard has been taken into community use, elsewhere planning policies have been made more sympathetic and old festivals revived - all because people have re-discovered their richness while making a Parish Map. In the process people have discovered each other, new ways of looking and been emboldened to argue their point of view with the professionals.

Many maps have been turned into posters and postcards, or have led to books, games, calendars, diaries and videos all of which have helped the map to reach many more people and generated income that can be put directly into the place. The poster of Uplyme in Devon, one of the first Parish Maps to be made, has been reprinted several times and has sold many thousand to people from the village and to many friends the other side of the globe. Attachment to locality is understood in most cultures. Parish Maps offer a means to socially express this, and to suggest ends - jobs for everyone to help sustain nature and culture and how you want them to meet in your place.

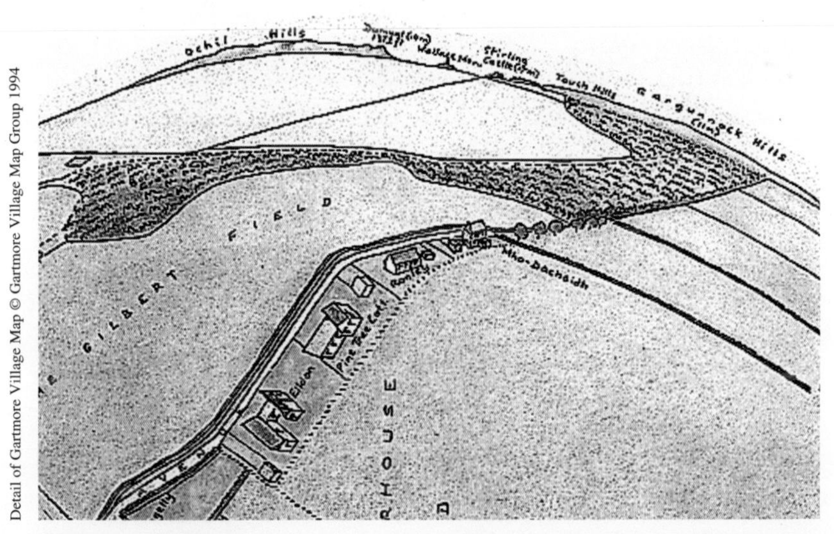

Gartmore, nr Stirling

"The official decision was to adopt a fish-eye lens. The map is a bird's eye view of the village. I like to think that it shows what many of us feel, that Gartmore is the centre of the known world! We are surrounded by stunning scenery and much unspoiled land - seen at its best on our few dry days." (printed on two sides, approx 3'x3')

AN EXPLORATORY ALPHABET FOR LOCAL DISTINCTIVENESS

Ayrshires, ammonites, ash trees, Arbor Day, allotments, avenue **B**arns, bluebells, bee skeps, birchwood, Branwen, bourne, beck, brook, burn, backlane, Bryanston plum, Charlotte Bronte, bridge, brewery, bonfire night, birthplace, the Black Dog, bulrushes, beacon, boundary, Brakspear's, beech hedge, badger sett **C**ream teas, crowstep gables, chalk figure, chine, coppice, clint, cobbles, caves, Constable, Carnival, cob, cairn, church bells, cooling towers, crannog, Cockney, combe, chicory, chimneys, Collywestons, crane, crinkle-crankle wall, corrie, croft, cliffs **D**owns, dewpond, Dorset Horn, dales, doors, drystone walls **E**mmets, elms, English bond, Eleanor cross, Eccles cakes, Elgar **F**ence, fen, flint, fieldnames, Foggathorpe, French Lieutenant's Woman, fells, fuchsia, foghorn **G**roynes, gates, gargoyle, gravel pit, gospel oak, granite kerbstone, Geordie, genius loci, gasometer, glen, garth, glowworm **H**ardy, hopfield, hornbeam, harbour, holm oak, hillfort, haymeadow, heath, hanger, Ham stone, honeysuckle **I**nbye islands **J**ackdaws, juniper, jetties, Jack o Kent **K**ent cobs, knapped flints, kirk, keld, kelp kilns **L**ong barrow, lynchet, loch, longhouse, lichen, lane, Lambton Worm, links, leat, level crossing, lapwings, London plane, D.H.Lawrence **M**ilestone, moor, marsh marigold, mazzard, Mayday, mizmaze, mullion, miners, mere, millstone grit, mosque, machair, may bug, mistletoe, market place, mist, maltings, milkchurn stand, March hare, monkey puzzle, **N**orfolk Beefing, newts, Nant y derry **O**ld Man's Beard, oast house, orchard, oilseed rape **P**it tip, ptarmigan, parish, pier, pargetting, peat bog, pantiles, pollarded willows, pigeon loft, pub sign, park, pavement, picnic place, plock, pillbox, Padstow obby oss **Q**uarry, quoin **R**ain, rockrose, railings, roofs, red soil, ridgeway, Robin Hood, rookery, railway, ruin, rath **S**unken lane, sand dunes, Staffordshire blues, snottygogs, stilton, Scots Pine, stile, strawbales, shopfront, seawall, standing stone, street market, spire, Scouse, slate, scarecrow, steelworks, square, starlings, shingles, scowles, stargazy pie **T**ottergrass, twitchel, tor, tarn, tithe barn, tower, Tamworths, thatched walls, towpath, terrace, tump, Tan Hill Fair,.red telephone box **U**ndercliff, Up helly-aa **V**alerian, village green, viaduct **W**eatherboard, watercress beds, warehouse, well-dressing, walkmill, wassailing, wind, weld, wold, wild raspberries **Y**ew, yellowbrick, Yorkshire pudding, y filltir sgwar **Z**eitgeist, Zennor...

Creating an alphabet together of things particular to your place can draw everyone in, the more detailed it becomes in words and pictures the more local distinctiveness it will capture.

The Practical Page

Talking to other Parish Mappers is the best ways of getting started, learn from their successes and mistakes. Common Ground has a list of Parish Maps reproduced for sale and can tell you of other groups in your area, please send an SAE.

Don't let a lack of cash stop you, many maps have been produced on nothing. However Common Ground has a list of suggested funders, please send an SAE. Try your County or District Council - Environment, Parish Paths, Planning, Arts, Agenda 21, Rights of Way, Countryside officers for grants and help.

Rural Action give grants for Parish Maps, to be used for hiring local experts, training, materials and printing. For a list of county contacts write to: Rural Action, Somerford Court, Somerford Road, Cirencester, Gloucestershire GL7 1TW

To help you discover your footpaths and boundaries contact the Footpaths Officer in your local authority, the Ramblers Association, 115 Wandsworth Road, London SW8 2XX or obtain a Rights of Way Action Pack from the Countryside Commission, Parish Paths Partnership, Crescent Place, Cheltenham, Gloucestershire GL50 3RA.

Remember, if you are planning to reproduce any part of an O. S. map on your Parish Map you have to pay a copyright fee. They produce their own leaflet on this: write to Ordnance Survey, Romsey Road, Southampton SO16 4GU for a copy of Copyright 2.

Common Ground has a laminated panels display 'Know Your Place - make a map of it', a video 'Holding Your Ground', and a slide pack. All offer practical help on getting started and are available for hire, send an SAE for details.

Other helpful publications from Common Ground:
Parish Maps leaflet, free with an SAE, or £1 for 10
from place to PLACE, maps and Parish Maps, ed. Sue Clifford & Angela King, Common Ground, 1996, £10

Ask Common Ground about Tree Dressing Day, Field Days and Apple Day, all are ways of getting started or keeping going.

Please let Common Ground know about your Parish Map, the best way to promote the project is by example and we can only do this with your help.

Thirsk Parish Map ©Thirsk Civic Society 1989

photo: Ian Carstairs, Countryside Commission

All photos by Common Ground, unless otherwise credited. Text by Beatrice Mayfield & Sue Clifford. Design by Stephen Turner. Printed on Sylvancoat, 100% recycled paper, by Wincanton Print, Somerset
ISBN 1 870364 15 5 Charity no. 326335.

We are grateful for the support of: The Barbican Centre, Carnegie UK Trust, Department of the Environment Environmental Action Fund, Local Government Management Board, London Boroughs Grants Committee & Rural Action

Common Ground, Seven Dials Warehouse
44 Earlham Street, London, WC2H 9LA **£2.50**